Maverick

– HAROLD PERKINS –

An environmentally friendly book printed and bound in England by
www.printondemand-worldwide.com

Mixed Sources
Product group from well-managed
forests, and other controlled sources
www.fsc.org Cert no. TT-COC-002641
© 1996 Forest Stewardship Council

FSC

PEFC

PEFC/16-33-415

PEFC Certified
This product is
from sustainably
managed forests
and controlled
sources
www.pefc.org

This book is made entirely of chain-of-custody materials

www.fast-print.net/store.php

Maverick
Copyright © Harold Perkins 2012

ISBN 978-178035-337-1

First Published 2010
Second Edition Published 2012 by
FASTPRINT PUBLISHING
Peterborough, England.

Contents

My First Education

I suppose I should start at the beginning. But I will start by telling you what sticks in my mind, not the first thing I remember.

When I was about eight years old, I lived in a back-to-back house, one up, one down. There were a sitting room, one bedroom, and an outside toilet. Although there was only one bedroom my sister and brother, myself and my mother slept in the same room – my sister, Sheila, in one bed, my brother, Tommy, in another bed, while I slept with my mother.

I can remember being woken about six thirty in the morning by the bed shaking violently. I was terrified. When I woke fully and opened my eyes all I could see was a big man with ginger hair on top of my mother. I screamed, as I thought something bad was happening, and I got a smack across my face and was told, 'Shut up you little bastard and go back to sleep.' With this I hid under the bedclothes, a blanket with a couple of army coats on top, and had to listen while he finished what I had interrupted. I later found out they called him Harry Allen. He was a night watchman at a local mill, and when he finished his night shift he would call and give my mother one before he went home to his wife. So that's not the first thing I remember, but something that stayed in my mind.

It was not to be the last time I would see this guy. He would turn up on a weekend – and he hated my guts. Any chance or excuse to give me a belt round the lughole and he was there.

We had an outside loo with a brick missing above the door. I assume this was an early form of ventilation. One Saturday I had been on our weekly shoplifting spree with a good friend who was slightly older than me, and we had got a great result, so I celebrated by going into our outside loo and smoking a Willie Woodbine. Yes, I was only eight years old. Mother saw the smoke coming out of the ventilation hole and instantly dragged me out across the cobbled yard and into the house. It must have been wintertime, because we had a big Yorkist range fireplace. This was a big cast-iron fireplace with an oven on one side and a tank to put water in on the other, so when you lit the fire the heat from the burning coals would heat up the water and the oven. It was throwing plenty of heat out. 'This little sod's been smoking,' said my mother to Harry Allen and my cousin Betty, who was twenty years older than me and more a mate to my mother than her niece.

'I'll cure the little bastard,' said Harry Allen, and he sent our Betty round to Fisher's shop for ten Woodbine. Back she came with the Woodbines and gave them to him. 'Right,' he said. 'We'll see if you like smoking.' He sat me right in front of the roaring fire on an orange box and put a Willie Woodbine in my mouth. After smoking a full one I thought that would be it but, no, in went another, and this time he said, 'Do the swallow.' So as not to be beat I took a drag on the cig and actually swallowed a mouthful of smoke. After doing this twenty odd times sat in front of the roaring fire I turned green and was sick in the stone sink at the top of the cellar steps. I thought after being sick that would be the end of it – wrong again.

'Right, you little bastard, are you going to stop smoking?' said Harry Allen. Well, being a stubborn little bastard (I think I took after my mother), I said, 'No, I will not stop smoking.'

I thought, This big ginger bastard who is giving my mother one and smacking me across the face is not telling me what to do. So back to the orange box. By this time it had been moved closer to the fire, which had been stoked up. After I had smoked the rest of the Woodbines, and being sick a few more times, again it was, 'Right you little bastard, are you going to stop now?' To which the answer was, 'No.' I must have been stupid.

'I'll cure you this time,' said Harry Allen. He pulled out a big wooden pipe filled with some horrible-smelling pipe tobacco and puffed on it until it was glowing. He shoved the wet end in my mouth and said, 'Smoke that and swallow every mouthful' – which I did, being sick only once. After about thirty minutes I thought I was dying. My mouth was sore and my tongue was burning.

'Right, you little bastard, are you going to say sorry for smoking?' I had been sick and was stood at the top of the cellar steps. 'Are you going to say sorry?' Harry Allen was yelling.

'No, I'm not.'

At that he put his foot in my back and kicked me down the cellar steps.

'There was no need for that.' That was the first time my mother had said anything. I still carried on smoking.

Another of my mother's friends was a coalman. Everyone in our yard could afford only one or two bags of coal when the coalman came every two weeks, but my mother always used to get five bags. When the coalman came to deliver the five bags with his mate, my mother would say, 'I want you to stand at the back of the wagon and count every bag he tips down the coal chute.' This was a mission for me – if he was going to fiddle us out of a bag of coal I was going to catch him out. The saying comes to mind, 'It takes a thief to catch a thief', and he was not going to outsmart this eight-year-old smartarse. So I was stood at the back of the wagon while the coalman's mate tipped the first bag down the coal chute. He shook all the coal dust down the chute and I thought, At least he's not leaving any coal in the bag to snaffle later. He folded the sack in half, walked to the back of the wagon, smoothed it out, then put a half-hundredweight block on top of it.

'Can't have them blowing away, can we?' he said. I thought, This guy's very efficient. With this he sat on the back of the wagon, pulled out a cig and tapped it on his cig packet for about four or five seconds before he lit it. I can remember thinking, That must make them taste better, I'll try that next time I have a smoke. So I stood watching the coalman's mate having a smoke when I should have been counting the bags of coal he was putting down the chute. I was just about to go down the passage to tell my mum that this guy had put only one bag of coal down the chute when he said, 'I'm starting again now,' so I didn't tell my mum. By the time he had climbed on the wagon and moved the sack to the edge, about fifteen minutes had gone by. Only when the coalman came back and the rest of the coal went down in about four minutes did I realise the coalman's mate had been stalling for time while the coalman was giving my mother one. This was how we could afford five bags of coal and everyone else could only afford one or two bags.

Another of my mother's friends was a guy called Jack Bane, who lived off Otley Road. Sometimes we would go down and see him at his house. He used to say to me, 'I'm going to teach you to box, and we will start off by shadow boxing.' He would spend a couple of minutes teaching me to shadow box, then he would say to me, 'To be a boxer you have to do some running, but slow running, not fast. I want you to set off and run to the end of the street, down Otley Road, up Barkerend Road, up Undercliffe Street then back on this road, but run slow. If you want to be a boxer you must run slow.' The slow run took about half an hour. When he came to our house it was a slow run down Lapage Street, on Leeds Road, up Killinghall Road. It wasn't until years later I worked out why I went on these slow runs, but I suppose it was better than counting coal sacks.

Every Saturday at Bradford Moor was bath time. We had a big tin bath and it was placed in the middle of the room near to the Yorkist range fireplace that had a place at the side to heat the water up. So with this boiler on the side of the fire and a few pans of water placed on the grille at the front of the fire the bath would eventually be filled. First of all in went Mother. We had to play out for half an hour while she soaked in the bath, then our Sheila went in after my mother. Again we had to play out. When it was our Tommy's and my turn the water was a bit cloudy and cold, although my mother always used to top it up with the hot water from the fire. I often used to wonder what it would be like to get a bath with nice clean water.

The first time I can remember having a bath on my own and not sharing the dirty water with someone else, I would have been about eleven years old. I had just gone to Tyersal School and palled up with a couple of lads who were in the same class as me. One was called Harry Long and the other one Billy Coathill. They went around together and I made friends with them. One Saturday afternoon I called round to see Harry Long. His dad was a coalman who worked for himself. Although they had a small house like ours (there were only three of them), it was posh to me. They had nice furniture but, like us, they didn't have a bathroom.

Harry's granddad ran a public house a stone's throw from where he lived, and they had a bathroom. When I called at Harry's house, his mum said, 'He's round at the pub getting a bath – why don't you go round and wait for him.' I toddled round to the back of the pub. They had a big yard and, to my amazement, a monkey in a cage. I had never seen a live monkey so close up. I knocked on the back door and Harry's grandmother opened it. I told her that his mum had told me to come round and wait for him while he had his bath. She asked me in and gave me a glass of pop and I asked her if it was a tin bath that they had. She had a chuckle at this and said, 'No, come with me,' and took me upstairs to the bathroom. By this time Harry had had his bath and was dressed. She opened the door of the bathroom and there was a big bath, not a tin one. This had taps on, one for hot and one for cold.

She said to me, 'Would you like to have a bath?'

'Yes, please,' I said. I couldn't believe my luck – a bath on my own in clean water. I thought I was dreaming. Sadly, the next week it was back to the tin bath and dirty water.

When it was summertime we didn't have the fire going even though we still had lots of coal in the cellar to heat the water. So every other Saturday my mum would send our Tommy and me over to Lapage Street slipper baths. For sixpence you could get a bath in nice clean water, although I still had to share with our Tommy because it was two for the price of one. One week we thought we'd skip the slipper baths and have sixpence to spend. At the time you could get five Woodbines and a box of matches and still get a halfpenny change, so we went without a bath and spent the money on ciggies. When we got home, we encountered 'Creeping Jesus' – that was our nickname for Mum, as she could lift the sneck on the door at the bottom of the bedroom steps and creep up the stairs and catch us doing something we shouldn't be doing, like smoking, or eating some sweets or chocolates we had nicked from Fisher's shop. We could never hear her coming, hence 'Creeping Jesus'. She said, 'You haven't been to the slipper baths.' As much as we insisted we had, she knew we hadn't. It wasn't until she said, 'Why isn't your hair still wet?' that we knew she was smarter than us. So the next time we put our heads under the water tap in the school playground to get our hair wet so it was still damp when we got home. I still think she had her suspicions.

I can remember being awakened by our Tommy, when we both slept in the same bed, and he said, 'Can you hear all the commotion?' I could hear people shouting and screaming then it went quiet. When we got up in the morning to go to school, there was blood outside our house and on the pavement, through the passage and down to the lamp post, where there was a big pool.

Our Tommy said, 'This is where he must have stopped and leaned against the lamp post.'

'Who?' I said.

'Alfred May,' replied our Tommy. When it all came out, my father – whom I had not seen because he had been abroad fighting for his country – had been demobbed. He had arrived home to find Alfred May in his bed with my mother (they had the bed downstairs) so my father had dragged Alfred May out of the house and given him a good hiding.

I never used to see my father because he thought he was not my father. He was always friendly with our Sheila and Tommy, but never with me. I grew up not knowing that my father had rejected me, thinking someone else had fathered me. When I was at school and all the kids used to talk about their fathers taking them out or playing football or cricket with them, I used to say my father had been killed in the war, so they never asked awkward questions.

My mother's friend Marjorie Butson lived a stone's throw away from us. One day she said to me, 'I saw you with your dad yesterday.'

I said, 'No, I don't even know what he looks like.'

'You were stood at the tram stop with him near Sparrow Park yesterday,' said Marjorie.

When I thought about it, there had been a man stood next to me while I was waiting for a tram to go into Bradford centre to see my probation officer, but I had no idea it was my father and he probably had no idea who I was. So I never saw him, and he never saw me, until our Tommy's fiftieth birthday celebration. They were having a party for him at a pub on Rooley Lane, and myself and Sandra were invited. We went in the pub and up to the bar to order our drinks.

Sandra said to me, 'Just look at that man sat at the bar in the other room.' The bar served two rooms, so you could see into the other room. 'He is the spitting image of you.'

So we went round to the other room, went up to the guy sat at the bar, and I said, 'Are you Kenneth Perkins?'

He said, 'Yes, and you must be Harold, nice to meet you.'

So at the age of forty-five, I had finally met and talked to my father, who is my spitting image. I still cannot muster up the courage to call him Dad.

Since I have got to know him he has told me a few tales, including about the time he gave Alfred May a good hiding. He said it wasn't the fact that he had been in bed with my mother, but that he had been wearing my father's suit that had upset him more.

So that's a few memories of some of my mother's 'boyfriends' at Coach Row, Bradford Moor, Bradford. There were more to come.

I suppose if you have read this far into the book you probably think I have been slagging my mother off or saying she was a bad mother. She wasn't bad, but she was very strict with us, and when she said something she meant it.

Just after World War Two, when my father was still in Burma waiting to be demobbed, she had to bring up three kids on her own, and that could not have been easy for her. Our Tommy and I were proper bad lads, so I suppose all the hidings we got were deserved.

As well as looking after three kids she worked evening shift at a local mill from five thirty until nine thirty. This was the time we would smuggle our contraband up to the bedroom and hide it for future access.

The house, even though it was a run-down back-to-back, was always kept clean and she would yellow stone the doorstep once a week. I could never fathom out why.

So all in all she was a good mother, despite her bringing home a new dad or new uncle now and again.

A Liar and a Thief

I was going to call this chapter 'The Naughty Boy', but then I changed it because some people I know, who live in Cyprus, reminded me of what I was like when I was a kid: a liar and a thief. I had an excuse. It was the way I was brought up. They all should have known better. I was brought up rough because my mother had mouths to feed plus herself and because it was after the war – food was on ration.

Money was very scarce, so I used to go over to the garden allotments, pull up the cabbage, carrots and potatoes, and then take them home so we had something to eat the next day. I suppose I knew it was wrong, but I was told to do it and, to be quite honest, I enjoyed it. Another source of food at Bradford Moor was a place a bit further away. It was at the edge of the golf course. It was a naughty boys' hostel and they called it 'Crow Trees'. This hostel had an orchard with lots of apple trees, blackberry bushes, and a greenhouse with tomatoes and grapes. They also had about twenty free-range hens that laid their eggs in the grounds of the orchard. This was like being let loose in Morrison's supermarket for fifteen minutes to grab a load of food. First it was the best apples we could reach – we always took a kitbag or a knapsack – then it would be a few blackberries, then into the greenhouse for the tomatoes and the grapes, then last of all the eggs. These hens had their own little nests to lay their eggs and over the months we had found them all. Some laid more eggs than others. If there were three eggs in one nest, two in another, we would leave the one with one in, take one out of the one with two in, and take two out of the one with three in. Same with the tomatoes – we never took so many that they would be missed. Or so we thought.

One Saturday afternoon we were on our shopping trip with our kitbag. We had done the greenhouse and the blackberries, put the kitbag behind a bush, and were collecting some eggs, when we were ambushed by the screws and some of the boys from the hostel. We had about five or six eggs each, which they took from us while giving us a telling off. We told them it was the first time we had taken the eggs, but I don't think they believed us, as I heard one of the screws saying to the other one, 'I thought for the last few months those hens have not been laying well. Now we know why.' They never did spot the kitbag with the tomatoes, grapes and blackberries in. We went back for our swag when we thought things had quietened down.

About the same time my brother, Tommy, said, 'Shall we break into the woodwork section at Lapage Street School?' This was a step up the ladder from pulling up spuds and carrots. I climbed on the roof, through a window and opened a door to let our Tommy in. We had a scout round, but before we could snaffle anything we heard the caretaker turning his key in another door. So we crept back to the door we had come in. As soon as the caretaker went through his door we ran out of the other, chased up the school yard by the caretaker, who was shouting, 'I know who you are!'

Within the hour the police were at our house and we were taken into custody for questioning. When it came to court our Tommy, who had been up in court a few times, said, 'If I am found guilty again they will send me down. Will you say I was in the school yard and that I didn't know you was inside the woodwork section?'

So when we went to court I said I was on my own, and that my brother was in the school yard. The caretaker said he had seen both of us coming out of the door, and the prosecutor, or whatever they called him at the time, said, 'So your brother Tommy would be in front of you, am I right?'

'Yes, he was.'

Prosecutor: 'Then how is it the caretaker says he saw you climb over the school wall first, if your brother was in front of you?'

I thought, this guy is trying to make a liar out of me, which I was, so I said, 'The reason I got to the top of the yard first was that I am a faster runner than my brother,' at which all of the court laughed, except the prosecutor.

For breaking into Lapage Street woodwork section I was sentenced to two years probation. Our Tommy was found not guilty. So for the next two years I had to walk once a week from Bradford Moor to Chapel Street probation office in the centre of Bradford and back again – approximately four miles.

My probation officer was called Mr Brown. One day (I think it was a Saturday) I saw his car outside our house. Thinking I was in trouble I ran into the house to see what was going on. When I got in, my mother said, 'Mr Brown wants to adopt you. What do you want to do?' Well, I was gobsmacked and didn't know what to say. My mother said, 'Go play out for half an hour and think about it.'

So I went and had a word with our Tommy. He said, 'If you go with Mr Brown he will send you to a posh school and you will end up talking posh.' I thought, I don't want to talk posh, so I said no. Years after, I thought, How can you ask an eight-year-old if he wants to be adopted?

It turns out Mr Brown was a very nice man. He once looked at my school report; out of thirty-six in the class I was second to bottom and the comment from my teacher was, 'Harold has the ability to do better, must try harder.' Mr Brown said, 'Next time if you get in the top ten I will give you ten shillings [fifty pence] and if you get to the top of the class one pound.' That was a fortune. Needless to say I came joint top, and true to his word Mr Brown gave me a crisp one-pound note. Good old Mr Brown. He knew how to get the best out of me.

A lady friend of my mother's called Auntie Annie – she was no relation but that is what we had to call her – lived down Otley Road area near to Jack Bane, and used to invite us down for Sunday lunch. This always consisted of what tasted like stew with a crust on top. I think she called it meat and potato pie. If it didn't have a crust it was the same, but with dumplings, and you had to eat the lot.

There would be me, Tommy and Mum. We would go to see Annie on Sunday afternoons and Mum would say, 'Best behaviour, and keep your hands in your pockets.' This meant we had not to nick anything. We sat down at the table and our Tommy said, 'I can't eat anything, I feel sick.' Auntie Annie was in the kitchen and my mum whispered, 'Tommy, eat it or you will offend Auntie Annie.' With this our Tommy got up from the table, rushed outside and was sick. I had a few spoons of stew and Mum said, 'Go see what is up with him,' so I went outside to see how he was doing. He was leaning over the wall retching. I went back in the house and got our Tommy a mug of water and took it out to him. By now he was sat on the wall. I gave him the water and he said, 'I can't eat that stew. I saw her getting it out of the oven and it was in the pee pot. She's made the stew in the pee pot that goes under the bed.' This took some believing, so when I took the pot that had the water in back to the kitchen I had a look round while they were all sat at the table. Sure enough, there was the pee pot with some stew in the bottom. 'Harold, come and finish your dinner,' shouted mum. I dared not disobey so I sat at the table looking at the stew and thinking about the pee pot. 'Come and eat your dinner,' Mum said in a tone of voice that meant, do as I say or... I said, 'It's cold.' Mum said, 'If you hadn't spent all that time outside it wouldn't be. Now eat it.' I looked at the stew and thought about the pee pot. There was only one thing to do. I got out of the chair, dashed out of the door, and ran like hell down the street. I made my way to Bradford Moor Park where I knew I would see some mates.

I spent a few hours in the park because I knew I would get a belt when I got home, but I thought I would sooner have the belt than Sunday lunch made in a pot that Auntie Annie had peed in.

I waited outside the post office where I could see the clock. When it got to six fifty-five I thought I had better get home. It was only three or four minutes' walk and I didn't want a double belting for being late as well as running off. When I got home and the door was open, I knew I wouldn't have to sleep in the outside loo, but I would get the belt. I thought of running straight up the stairs to bed – I might escape a belting. No chance. 'Come here, you little bastard. You made me look a fool and showed me up this afternoon at Auntie Annie's.'

When we got a belting we used to hide under the table so she couldn't get a full swing at us. Whoever cried first was a sissy, so we would start laughing, but the more we laughed the more we got belted. This time I was on my own and I wasn't laughing.

'Why did you run off?' asked Mum.

'I wasn't eating stew made in a pee pot,' said I.

Mum said, 'Auntie Annie is a very clean lady, and had broken the bowl she normally does the stew in, and she scalded the pee pot out before she used it. Now, get to bed. I'm not taking you out again on a Sunday.' Thank God for that, no belting and no pee-pot pie to eat again.

Before every Christmas my mother used to threaten us and say, 'If you don't behave yourselves you'll get cinders in your stocking on Christmas Day and nothing else.' We always used to hang our stockings at the bottom of the bed, and we always got an apple and orange and a mixture of nuts in the stocking for when we woke on Christmas morning. But one time me and our Tommy had been very naughty and sure enough she stuck to her word. We woke up, and there were our stockings at the bottom of the bed full of cinders. It was quite a shock. It was well into the afternoon before she let us have the apple and orange and the mixed nuts.

It was only around Christmas time that we would get the special treats, like butter on our bread. We normally had margarine, so butter was a luxury. Another treat was Nestlé milk on buttered bread but, when we didn't have the butter or the margarine to put on it, my mum used to spoon it straight on to the dry bread. If you weren't quick at picking it up, the Nestlé condensed milk would seep through the dry bread and would stick to the tablecloth, which was usually a copy of the Telegraph and Argus newspaper. This meant if you turned your bread upside down you could read last week's news.

It was around this time just after Christmas that me and our Tommy bought an HMV wind-up gramophone, with two 78 rpm records, for two shillings and sixpence – half a crown, or twelve-and-a-half pence in the new money. One of the records was 'Mule Train'. We played it over and over. One day Hetty Overfield, who lived on the Green, said, 'I'll give you seven shillings and sixpence for it,' so our Tommy said yes, and collected the money. I was looking forward to my share of the profit, but never got it. I was learning all the time.

My mother was very strict with our Sheila, Tommy and me, but she seemed to mellow a little as the rest of the family came along.

I can remember one time at Bradford Moor; it was a Sunday tea time, and Alfred May was there. We were all sat round the table. If you wanted a slice of bread you had to ask Mother, who would cut it for you – no sliced bread then. Because Alfred May was there we had butter on the table – yes, butter, not margarine.

Alfred May said to my mother, 'I'll have a slice of bread please, with butter on, and when I say butter I mean butter.' So my mother cut him a slice of bread and spread the butter on. She normally used to spread it on then scrape it off. So when I wanted a slice of bread, I said, 'Can I have a slice of bread, please, with butter on – and when I say butter I mean butter.' Now, it was OK for Alfred May to say that, but not me. She knocked me off the chair and dragged me up the stairs to the bedroom. It was about four thirty and I knew what it meant: it meant I was in bed without any tea or supper and I couldn't play out, all because I said the same as Alfred May.

Come next morning I was up and ready for school. It was always the same, a cup of tea and one slice of jam and bread, but not for me this time. Mother said, 'Are you going to say sorry?' I thought, Why should I say sorry when Alfred May said it? He didn't get into trouble. Now, because I wouldn't say sorry, I didn't get my cup of tea and a slice of jam and bread. I got put in front of me my Sunday tea that was still on the plate and stale. 'That's what you are getting until you say you're sorry,' said the old girl. I wouldn't eat it, I wouldn't say sorry, so I went to school minus breakfast.

Twelve o'clock came. The bell rang and I was out of school and on my way home for dinner. On a Monday it was usually a stew or what was left from Sunday with some bits added to make it go further, but not for me. No, it was my Sunday tea again, there on the table waiting for me. Now all I had to do was say sorry and I could have had some stew, but I was just as stubborn as my mother and I wouldn't give in. So for three days' breakfast, dinner, tea and supper, it was stale Sunday tea which never got eaten. I didn't starve. I nicked some carrots from the allotments and some broken biscuits from Driver's the grocer's shop, and begged a bit of bread from my mates. It was Wednesday tea before she let me have something to eat. Would I never learn?

When Old Year's Night came – or New Year's Eve as some people call it – it was time to go 'first footing' and earn some money. What we would do was go round and knock on people's doors and wish them a happy new year and give them a piece of black coal for good luck. It always worked. They were in a good mood, and at ten o'clock at night they had probably had too much to drink and were generous with their money, especially when you gave them this big shiny black lump of coal.

Sometimes they would give you a sixpence or a shilling not knowing that the coal had come from their coal shed at the bottom of their garden – and if their shed was locked we would go back to one we knew

23

was open. Another good earner; pity it only came once a year.

It would be about 2 a.m. I was being chased by about eight or nine policemen and a couple of Alsatian dogs. I can remember running down the driveway of a big house. The police and their dogs were getting closer, when all I saw in front of me was a ten-foot-high wall and nowhere else to go. I thought, I'll never get over that wall, but I was not a quitter. When you've got those dogs snapping at your ankles it gives you added incentive.

I ran up the wall and just managed to grab the top and haul myself up and over to the other side. It was too high for the police and their dogs to get over, and the drop at the other side was into a field. So I set off running across the field.

By this time the police had gone round the big house and into the field by a gate. They brought their cars in and put the headlights on full beam, scanning the field for me. I was down flat on my stomach and crawling in the grass. When they shone their lights to where I was lying, I kept perfectly still. I could feel and hear my heart pumping at a lively pace and I only moved when they shone the lights away from me. Eventually I came to a stream. It was about three feet down in the field, six or seven feet across, and a couple of feet deep. I slid down the bank and put my head up to see where the police were. They were heading straight towards me with their dogs, and were about 1,000 feet away.

I could remember seeing a film about an escaped convict in America, being chased by the police with bloodhounds. The character in the movie broke off a reed from the side of the river and lowered himself into the water. He then went under the water and breathed through the reed that he had put into his mouth with the other end just above the water to enable him to take air in. Now, not only were there no reeds about, this was a stream only two feet deep, not a river. Not to give in I lay in the stream, which was freezing cold, with just my nose above the water to enable me to breathe. I could hear the police coming with their dogs.

They passed within three feet of me and never saw me, and the dogs didn't get my scent. I gave them time to get well away before I emerged from my watery bed. It was a good two hours before they gave up and left me there, shaking and freezing to death. I thought afterwards, Would I have lain in the stream if I hadn't seen the film?

There was a grocer's shop at the corner of Lapage Street and Maidstone Street at Bradford Moor. The guy who ran it was a black man, a very nice obliging chap. His shop was packed full of everything. One day our Tommy and I paid him a visit. This particular week he had a special offer on Pear's soap. The only soap we ever saw was cut from a long green piece and they called it carbolic. The Pear's soap was situated at the right-hand side of the counter with the top of the box about one foot below the top of the counter.

The wall at the back was floor to ceiling in drawers that he kept goods in. The bestsellers were ground to eye level and the bad sellers right at the top. This meant that if you asked for something from the top drawer he had to go round the back where he was out of sight and get his ladders to gain access to the top drawers. Our Tommy's trick was to ask for something from one of the top drawers – then, when he went for his ladder, Tommy would fill his pockets with Pear's soap. When the shopkeeper came back with the ladder, our Tommy would say, 'Oh, I've left the money on the table at home. I'll be back in ten minutes.' And with this we would go out of the shop. It hadn't cost us anything and we had a dozen or so bars of posh soap which would be sold on at a reduced price with 100 per cent profit. I still can't remember getting my share.

Another of our Tommy's tricks was when he had a paper round for a shop down Amberley Street. In those days, if the milkman delivered and you weren't in when he came round to collect his money, you would leave the money with a note in an empty milk bottle. He would pick the bottle up and take his money out with the note. Well, he would if our Tommy hadn't got there before him. His trick was to drop the newspaper next to the milk bottle, put the bottle containing the money inside the paper and pick it up, drop the bottle and money into the paper bag, and then put the paper through the letterbox. He made more doing this than he got for delivering the papers. I think they eventually sussed him out, but couldn't prove anything. One more scam bites the dust.

One of the legal ways we had to make money was selling artificial flowers. My mother used to make flowers from coloured paper. She would cut shapes like petals, then put a blade of the scissors to the back of the petal and scrape the petal until it curled. Then she would fasten the petals together with some wire and put some more paper round the wire so it looked like a stem. When she had done it looked quite effective – a nice flower with different coloured petals. Then our Tommy and I would go round selling them by knocking on doors or standing outside a shop. I suppose it was just like the Gypsies selling pegs. Our Tommy didn't like doing this, so I was left to do all the leg work.

Another hobby of my mother's was tabbing rugs. This consisted of getting a big sack and giving it a good wash. Next you got a load of old different coloured clothes, which wasn't hard for my mother as we had a rag and bone man who lived in our yard.

You cut all the old rags and clothes up into four-inch by one-inch strips, then cut an arrow shape at each end. My mother used to draw a pattern on the sacking like a round ring in the middle, then some lines round the ring, and write 'red', 'black' or 'blue' or 'brown' on the lines. Then we all sat round the sacking with a thing called a tabber to make the holes in the sacking to put the tab through (a tabber was half a wooden clothes peg that had been sharpened at one end in order to pierce the sacking).

It was very boring, but if my mother said that you had to tab the rug that is what you had to do. When the rug was finished and you could see all the different colours in it, that was when you got the satisfaction for all the hours you had spent sticking the tabber through the sacking and not getting paid for it.

The Errand Boy

When I lived at Bradford Moor I used to run errands for the neighbours who were too old or too lazy to go to the shops for themselves. Or I would climb down the coal chute if they had locked themselves out. One next-door neighbour, a lady called Ann, used to call on me regularly, so I used to slide down the coal chute, up the cellar steps, have a quick scan round to see if I could snaffle a couple of ciggies from her packet, and then open the door. She would give me a threepenny bit (just over one pence in today's money). I would slip the threepenny bit in my hidden money box and when I got up to sixpence I would go up to the post office and buy a sixpenny saving stamp and put it in my book. When I had done that sixty times I would cash it in and collect one pound ten shillings (one pound fifty pence today).

As well as climbing down cellar grates and running errands, I had more things to boost my income. One was to take the empty pop bottles from the back yard of the off licence and go into the shop to get a penny each for returning the bottles. This was a good earner until the shop keeper rumbled us. Then what we would do was snaffle the bottles from the back yard, wait until a lad was going in the shop and say to him, 'Take these five pop bottles back and we will give you a penny.' This only worked about four times and we were rumbled again.

Another scam involved a shop down Barkerend Road. They sold Du Maurier cigarettes and kept them on the counter. The shopkeeper would sit in the back room and only come out when he heard the bell tinkle. When the door opened a small ball that was attached to a piece of string would make the bell tinkle, but if you opened the door only about five inches you could move the ball over and open the door without the bell sounding. So our Tommy used to do this, get in the shop, and help himself to five or six packets of Du Maurier – any more would have been missed. I would be outside the half-glass door keeping an eye out for anyone coming up to the shop. As soon as I saw our Tommy had got the cigs into his pockets I would open the door, the bell would tinkle, the shopkeeper would appear from the back room and we would ask for a halfpenny stick of Spanish, a small liquorice sweet. Hey presto! Six packets of cigs and a stick of Spanish all for a halfpenny. A nice little earner.

During the school holidays I used to go hunting for lost golf balls on Bradford Moor golf course and sell them to golfers for a few pence each. If they were new balls you could get sixpence each for them. I soon realised that if I hid in the long grass by the tenth hole, and waited until they hit their ball over the hill, where they could not see them, I could run out, snatch the nearest balls and jump over the fence before they got to the brow of the hill. You just had to remember not to try to sell the same balls back to the golfers you had snaffled them from.

Another little trick we would do was to climb over the wall into the builder's yard, where he kept about four hens. We would go where the hens were in cages and steal the eggs and fry them in candle fat when my mum was out. We dared not use Mum's lard because she always knew exactly how much she had. We could never have anything in the bedroom as my mother used to search us before we went to bed, so what we used to do to get things in the bedroom was hide the stuff in the outside loo. Then I would ask to go to the toilet where I would load the booty in a string bag. My mother always had lots of wool stored upstairs, so Tommy would make a rope out of the wool, open the bedroom window and lower the rope down. I would tie the bag on and he would pull it up. I would run back to the toilet, flush it, cross the yard and nip up to the bedroom where we would share the booty out. It might have been biscuits we had nicked from Driver's or sweets nicked from Fisher's shop. One time it was a bottle of wine our Tommy stole from the chemist. It was supposed to be medicinal: 'Hall's Fortified Wine'.

Sometimes my mother would get suspicious of me wanting to go to the toilet and she would tell me to go back up the stairs. So I invented my sleepwalking trick. I would go down the steps, open the door at the bottom and, with my eyes half open and my arms stretched out in front of me, with a slight groaning coming from my mouth, I would head towards the door that led to the toilet across the cobbled yard. The first time I did this, Alfred May was just about to grab me when my mother said, 'Don't touch him – he's sleepwalking.' She went in front of me and opened the door. The only trouble was I couldn't put any contraband in the bag for our Tommy to pull up because she was watching me from behind the curtains to make sure I didn't sleepwalk out of the toilet and down the road. After a couple of times when she knew I would be OK she stopped watching me and I could fill the bag up again. All went well until disaster struck. I had been sleepwalking to the toilet and had filled the bag up with the goodies. As our Tommy was pulling the bag up past the window it banged on the glass. Out came the old lady to confiscate our goodies and give me a belt round the lughole for making her think I was sleepwalking. And that was the end of this method of getting our stuff into the bedroom. It would be back to the drawing board to think of a better way.

We always tried to smuggle our contraband upstairs. We tried hiding stuff in our shoes, then putting a sock inside the shoe to cover it up. We even stashed the goods down our trousers near our private parts – but, no, you couldn't fool Creeping Jesus. She was too smart for us.

Our last idea was the best. With the house being old and the floorboards full of woodworm and gnawed away by the mice, it wasn't difficult to prise a floorboard up. We looked round for the shortest and easiest to pull up. It wasn't hard to do as we didn't have any lino or carpets down; it was just bare board. When we found a board we could remove and replace without it looking obvious we waited until Creeping Jesus was out of the house. We would then bring in our goodies and hide them under the floorboard. After Creeping Jesus had searched the bedroom and ourselves, which she now did every night, we could be assured of a feast once we were in bed. This again went well for weeks.

One time when we were getting some of our goodies from under the floorboards she could hear us. She was up the stairs like a flash. 'What are you two up to this time?' she said.

'Nothing, mum,' I said.

'I've heard some scuffling. What have you been doing?'

I said, 'I thought I heard some mice. She believed me, as she gave a grunt and went back down the stairs. We got away with it again.

Another weekly stunt was to climb on to the roof of the toilets up the back of Back Coach Row, over the wall and on to the roof of the out buildings to the Coach and Horses pub. From here I could climb through the bedroom window on to the hallway and down to the pub, where I used to help myself to several packets of ciggies and a couple of quid out of the float. I never took enough to be missed, as I used to do this little stunt every week until the landlady caught me hiding under the bed of her son, Peter. I got away with it because I told her that I had lent Peter a comic and he wouldn't give me it back, so I had come to find it myself. Luckily she let me go, otherwise it would have been another trip to the juvenile court and probation or approved school.

My job on a Saturday morning was to run the errands. For a kid of eight I had a very good memory. I could go to the shop and remember eight or nine items. It was only when it was a full shopping list that I had to take the list.

A grocer called Driver's was always my first stop. I used to give Harry, the manager, the list and, while he was getting the order, I used to ask if I could have a bag of broken biscuits as they cost only one penny for a bagful. He always said yes and would give me a blue bag to help myself. I would go along the line of biscuit tins to pick out the broken ones. If I got to the end of the tins and the bag wasn't full, I would work my way back along the line to break a few more to fill the bag up. Harry the manager used to say, 'I didn't think we had that many broken biscuits.' I'm sure he knew what I was up to.

My next stop would be Widdup's butchers, next to the Coach and Horses pub. I would go in there and tell him what I wanted. My mother always used to tell me to ask for some spare ribs for the dog, as he never charged for them if you said they were for the dog. So every week I would get the order and then say, 'Mum wants some spare ribs for the dog.' This went on for weeks and every Saturday night we used to have spare ribs for supper – great!

Everything went well until about four weeks later I went to the butcher's and gave him the order and said, 'My mum wants some spare ribs for the dog.'

'What do they call your dog?' he asked.

I was struck dumb and for the life of me could not think of a dog's name. After a few moments I said, 'Paddy,' as that was the name of my mother's friend Marjorie Butson's dog.

So Mr Widdup said, 'You haven't got a dog, have you?'

I said, 'No.'

Mr Widdup (I think he had known for a long time there was no dog) said, 'You can have them this week, but it's the last.'

So that was the end of the spare rib suppers, until about seven or eight weeks later when, after I had got the order, Mr Widdup said, 'Have you got a dog yet?'

I said, 'No.'

With that Mr Widdup said, 'Wait there.'

So I waited about five minutes and he gave me a parcel and said, 'That's just in case you get a dog.' Good old Mr Widdup – we could have spare ribs for supper!

For shopping purposes my mother always had two 'shopping accounts' as they were known then. One was at Driver's and one was at Jesse Stephenson's. She had a tick or credit book for each shop, take now, pay later. Inside the book would be a list of the goods that she had bought and opposite would be the price. At the bottom would be a total, and underneath the total amount she had paid that week. So if the total was one pound four shillings and sixpence, and she had paid one pound two shillings, she would still owe two shillings and sixpence to go on the next week's bill. She would play one off one against the other. If she owed Jesse Stephenson more than she could afford to pay, the manager would say to me, 'Tell your mother she will have to pay this off before she can have any more food on tick.' I would go home, tell Mum this, and then she would then send me to Driver's grocer's to pay some and tick some. This meant we didn't go short of food. The next week at Jesse Stephenson's she would send me with a few shillings to pay off the tick bill and just a few items to put on tick.

The manager would say to me, 'Where were you last week?' to which I had been told to answer, 'Because you wouldn't let us have any food until we paid, my mum sent me to Driver's for the week's groceries.' He would say, 'Tell your mother to send a full shopping list down,' so I would go back home, tell my mother this, and she would then take advantage of the situation and pile on the list. She knew that the manager at Jesse Stephenson's didn't want to lose out to Driver. There were no flies on my mother; there may have been a coalman or a night watchman or a soldier, but no flies.

Just round the corner from the Coach and Horses was a chip shop. We'd buy fish cake and chips when we could. Never a whole battered fish – that was a luxury we could not afford. It was my mum's favourite fish shop and I had to go there. Now, I had a liking for vinegar. When the fish shop guy had his back to me I used to reach up to the counter, grab the vinegar bottle, guzzle half a bottle down then put it back. He did eventually catch me and barred me from the fish shop. This meant I had to go to another fish shop, and my mother could tell the difference. Although I insisted I had bought the chips from the Coach and Horses fish shop, she would not have it, so I had to tell her I was barred for drinking the vinegar. With this information my mother dragged me up to the fish shop man, gave me a couple of cracks round the lughole, and with that I was allowed to go back to my mum's favourite fish shop. What a life!

It was a rainy day, and Keith Stocks and I were playing in the passage next to our back-to-back in Bradford Moor so we didn't get wet through. We were betting one another who could climb the highest by putting one hand and foot on one side of the passage wall and the other hand and foot on the other side. It was very hard work, especially when you were only small. Keith could always get higher than me. He was bigger and older and a lot stronger. This time I really tried my hardest and had climbed about six foot when Mr Donnelly came up the passage. Now Mr Donnelly was the local rag and bone man who lived in the corner house in our yard. When he had finished his rounds he would bring his horse and cart full of rags into the yard and he would always let my mother have first choice of the best rags that would nearly fit us. We were the best-dressed-off-a-rag-and-bone-cart in Bradford Moor.

Mr Donnelly was supposed to be deaf. Whenever you shouted after him he never responded, and even if you talked face to face with him he would shake his head and point to his ears. When he came through the passage, instead of just walking under me he gave me a tap on the leg and mumbled something to himself. I came down to the ground faster than I had gone up. I let him get to the end of the passage so he definitely couldn't hear me call him 'a silly old bastard'. This is when I found out he wasn't deaf. He came back and gave me a belt round the lughole.

In the school holidays we had to entertain ourselves, so in the summer months Keith Stocks and I used to go blackberry picking in Fagley Woods, which were about three miles away. But we made an adventure of it. First we would go into Bradford Moor

Park and climb the biggest trees. Keith was a tough kid. He loved doing things that were dangerous. We would climb the big trees in the park until the park warden saw us. He would sneak up, and as we were dropping from the last branch on the tree, he would whack us with his wooden cane stick. As soon as we got out of whacking distance we would call him names, then run off.

If we couldn't nick any pop from the shops on the way, Keith used to knock on the door of a house and ask for a cup of water as we were very thirsty and couldn't afford to buy any pop. Nine times out of ten it worked. If it was a woman she would feel sorry for us and give us glass of pop each. Another little trick I learnt.

On the way to Fagley Woods we would go through a council estate that was being built. Most of the workforce were prisoners of war. As we passed they would beckon us over and in broken English ask us if we would go to the shop and buy them some cigarettes. So we took the money off them and headed for the little green hut just before you get to Fagley Woods. Keith walked straight past the green hut, and I said, 'What about the cigs?' Keith said, 'You don't think we're spending the money on cigs? We can have two and sixpence each.' To which I instantly agreed, so we carried on to pick the blackberries.

Another one of my Saturday morning errands was to go to the dog meat shop for my posh Auntie Susan, my favourite auntie. She had a Great Dane called Bruce. When I stopped at her big house on a Saturday night and all day Sunday, I think it was another way of my mother getting me out of the way. I would go down to the horsemeat butcher and buy five shillings' worth for the dog. I would return home and my mother always used to open up the parcel of meat to inspect it. She would invariably say, 'This is too good to feed to a dog,' and proceed to remove the best bits, which later would be consumed by yours truly. So off I would go on my travels on a Saturday night from Bradford Moor to Shipley with the horsemeat for Bruce.

I would board a tram from Bradford Moor into the centre, Forster Square, and then another tram to Shipley, where my Auntie Susan would always greet me with a hug and a kiss and then take the dog's food from me. I loved going to visit Auntie Susan and my cousin Nigel. They lived in a big house with a garage, lounge, dining room, drawing room, three bedrooms and a big attic that was called 'The Studio'. This was where my Uncle Paul developed all his photographs of naked women – you can read about that later.

This was luxury. They even had butter and sugar, loads of it, as just after the war it was on ration. But because my Uncle Paul owned a few dance halls, he must have had the money and access to buy on the black market. He was also a member of the Magic Circle and used to invent tricks. When he made up a new trick he would show it to me only once and then ask me if I could fathom out how he had performed it.

He would give me a shilling (or five pence as it is now), which was a small fortune in those days. So I always put my little brain on overtime when he had a new one to show me. I can remember one. He would light a cigarette and puff on it until the end was glowing, insert the lit cigarette into his clenched left hand, open his hand with his knuckles facing me, then turn his hand round so I could see the palm of his hand – and the lit cigarette had disappeared, hey presto! I had to fathom out how it was done, so I said, 'It's gone up your sleeve.' He had a jacket on and it was the only thing I could think of. 'How did it get up my sleeve?' said Uncle Paul. I was thinking of the shiny shilling and my brain was buzzing. Uncle Paul said, 'I will give you half an hour to work it out.' I said, 'Show me it again,' but I knew he wouldn't, so I put my mind to it and came up with the idea that he must have had a small container hidden in the palm of his hand, otherwise the cigarette would have burnt him. So far so good; but how did it disappear? I thought he had put the lit cigarette into the container he had secreted in the palm of his hand then, when he turned his hand, he had dropped the container with the cigarette in it on the floor and stood on it while I was looking at his hand. But the trick was done and I wasn't sure if he had dropped it on the floor.

After about fifteen minutes, Uncle Paul said, 'Have you worked it out?' I said, 'I think I have, but I would like to see it again.' Now, Uncle Paul had never shown a trick twice, but he said, 'Just this time.' So he lit the cigarette, puffed on it until it glowed, inserted it into his clenched fist – and when he opened it I looked at the floor instead of his hand. Nothing, he did not drop it on the floor. Back to the drawing board.

I was still thinking of the shiny shilling and decided it must have gone up his sleeve. He must have had an elastic band tied to the container and then fastened near his shoulder. My thirty minutes was up, and Uncle Paul told me so. I said, 'It's up your sleeve, and you had some elastic fastened to something you put the cigarette into.' With this he put his hand in his pocket and gave me the shiny shilling. 'Yes, well done.' And he showed me the trick, revealing the small round metal container with the elastic band fastened to it.

Another trick he invented – but I never fathomed it out – was turning water into wine then back into water. This involved two wine glasses and a jug of water. One glass had a minute drop of metholated spirits in the bottom, so small you could not see it. The other glass had a very small tablet in – again you could not see it. When he poured the water into the glass with the metholated spirits in it, it turned to the colour of wine, and the second one with the tablet in would stay water-looking. Then he would pick up both glasses and pour them both together back into the jug and, once again, hey presto, water. This one baffled me. I just could not work it out. So he explained that the small amount of meths turned the water into wine; the tablets in the other glass when poured into the jug turned the wine colour back into water. Magic.

Bruce was like a pony to me, and Cousin Nigel and I used to ride the dog. Cousin Nigel used to climb on its back and off Bruce would go and give him a ride round the yard. When it came back I would climb on its back and say 'giddy up', but it wouldn't move and would growl at me. So I would dismount, if it hadn't thrown me off already, and give it a sly kick. Once I was playing in the garage when Bruce came galloping up to me. I was terrified that this massive dog was going to eat me up, so I picked up the yard brush and gave it a whack on the head, and off it went. It didn't bother me any more that weekend. But the next weekend I was playing indoors with Cousin Nigel because it was raining. Nigel was riding Bruce and fooling about with the dog. When I tried to get on its back it turned on me. It got hold of me by the head and shook and dragged me round the room until Auntie Susan pulled it off.

Uncle Paul put me in his car and drove me down to Salts Hospital at Saltaire, only five minutes away from Auntie Susan's. They stitched me up and put a bandage round my head. I can always remember Uncle Paul putting five pounds in the charity box. A big white fiver! To this day I have the scars from where the dog bit me. At the time my mother said they were not sure whether to put the dog down for biting me or have me put down for annoying the dog. They didn't have the dog put down. They just kept it out of my way or put me out of the dog's way. My mother always said that, because I had plonked it one with the yard brush in the garage, it never forgot. It was only getting its own back.

Uncle Paul's studio was a big attic where, as an amateur photographer, he used to develop the photos he had taken. It was out of bounds. Now, telling little Harold Perkins that on no account whatsoever was he to go up the attic stairs to Uncle Paul's studio was like asking a baby not to cry. I would have been about eleven years old at the time. My cousin Nigel and I were playing inside because of the rain. We were at the bottom of the attic stairs and I thought I would have a peep up in the studio. Cousin Nigel said, 'No, we can't go up there.' Now, Nigel was a few years younger than me and not quite as streetwise as yours truly, so I said to him, 'How many swear words do you know?' He said, 'None,' so I said to him, 'If you keep a look out for me I will learn you some swear words.' With this I was up the stairs like a rat up a drainpipe. My eyes popped out of their sockets when I saw all these photographs of nude women – not porno, just women posing with nothing on. Straightaway I thought, There's a few bob to be made out of this. I scanned through all the files of photos and some were duplicated. So down my jumper they went, about five or six. Down the steps I went, and taught Nigel a couple of swear words, 'sod' and 'bugger'. I thought I would save the naughtier ones for another time.

Monday morning at Tyersal School I was charging one penny a time to look at photos of ladies in the nude. When word got round, which didn't take long, I was making a lot of pennies. One of the lads asked if he could buy one for two shillings. I thought, to get two shillings I would have to show twenty-four people one photo. There was also a rumour going round that the teachers knew what was happening, so I began selling these photos of nude ladies for two shillings a time, teaching Nigel more swear words and making a few quid. For an eleven-year-old, cushty.

About twenty years later I saw a guy in a night club who said to me, 'Did you go to Tyersal School?' I said, 'Yes.' He said, 'You were the one who used to sell the nude photos?' Yes, all those years had gone by and he still remembered the photos.

When I was at Auntie Susan's I used to think I was in another world, because they were so rich. They had carpets and all the things that we never had. Cousin Nigel always had the latest Dinky toys and I was very envious of him. I didn't have any, so I used to pinch a few. I thought if he had all those and I had nothing it was all right for me to snatch some. Cousin Nigel then noticed he was a few Dinky toys missing and I was the only suspect. When I said I hadn't taken anything there was a search and I was guilty again. So when I couldn't steal any Dinky toys I used to nick the rubber tyres off them and hide them in my socks at the front. They noticed the tyres missing and the only suspect was searched. But they never thought to look in my socks – it was probably because my feet stank. The next day I would take them to school and sell them at half the price they cost in the Dinky toy shop.

A lady called Mrs Greenwood lived on Back Coach Row. Our Tommy used to run errands for her, and she always used to pay the price that ten Woodbine cigarettes cost (at the time about tenpence halfpenny – and when the packet went up to eleven pence, so did the errand money). When our Tommy went to the shop he took with him a list that Mrs Greenwood had given him. She used to say, 'Ask Mr Jubb to write the prices on the list.' Our Tommy was too wise to let the shopkeeper write the prices down. He used to write them in himself and would add half a pence on here and a penny on there. At the end of the bill, which probably consisted of a couple of dozen items, he would make as much as eight or nine pence on top of his errand money.

When our Tommy reached the age of being too old to run errands, I took over. 'Don't forget to doctor the bill,' said our Tommy. So I used to go to the shop with the list and remember the proper prices of the goods, then add the pennies and halfpennies on and put them on the list. I never thought of this, but my handwriting was a lot neater than our Tommy's. When I gave the list to Mrs Greenwood she said, 'Who served you?' I said, 'Mr Jubb.' 'That's strange. These numbers are a lot different to how he usually writes.' To this I said, 'Mr Jubb served me, but Mrs Jubb put the prices down.' 'Oh, I see,' said Mrs Greenwood. Phew, that was a close one. I was still learning.

I would be about nine or ten years old when my cousin Betty and her husband Jack (the one that although she was my cousin, she was more my mother's age) moved from one end of Clayton to the other, they had rented a council house that had a bathroom and an inside toilet, far better than the house they used to live in with no bathroom and the toilet was a walk of one hundred yards and if you got there and the council were emptying the toilet (it was a big dustbin and they came round every two weeks to empty it) you had to wait until they had done their job, so this new house was a novelty and my Mother and step Father had been invited to come and inspect the new house, I think it was a Saturday or a Sunday and they took me with them because no one would look after me (I can't think why) now their eldest was younger than me and I was told to look after John and play in the garden with him to keep him occupied and not let him out of the garden, now this was a novelty to me a garden, green grass and vegetables growing, when all I was used to was cobble stones with muck and grass between the cobbles, so for about half an hour it was different, but entertaining John I got bored and I was thirsty so I thought I would go for a drink of water, now in those days you didn't just go and put the mug under the tap, you had to ask "Please could I have a drink of water?" so I left John playing with his toys and went up to the side kitchen door, it was locked so I went round to the front door (two doors on one house?) that was locked now although I was only nine or ten years old my mind was a little older, instead of going back to play with John as most kids would have done I thought why would they lock all the doors? So I wandered round the outside of the house looking through all of the downstairs windows to see if I could attract some ones attention to get a drink of water, no chance, I looked through every window and saw nobody, because I could not see anyone I assumed that they had all gone out maybe to the local pub, so I went round the back of the house where the kitchen window was and noticed it was opened a few inches at the top, so with great difficulty and the help of some garden implements I managed to climb onto the window sill and could just manage to pull the top window down enough so I could climb through, now don't forget I thought that they had all gone out to the local pub and was quite surprised when I climbed through the window to hear noises coming from upstairs, now don't forget I just couldn't help myself to a mug of water I had to ask, so up the steps I went and could hear strange noises, nine or ten years old I didn't think and opened the bedroom door now there were two men and two women half dressed, I'll never know to this day whether I caught them before or after the swapping I will never know, all I know is I got a good hiding from my Mother for disturbing them while they were trying each other's clothes on. This 'friendly' banter must have been going on for a while because when they lived in their old house we once stopped over on a Saturday night and it was only a one bedroom cottage and all four slept in the same bedroom and I slept on the couch in the living room and could not get to sleep for what I thought was laughing and joking.

Up to No Good Again

Because I was young and had been brought up rough the police were always knocking on our door, now we only had one door in our back to back house, but when the police knocked at our door and asked to speak to little Harold Perkins I found a back door, I think the first time it was when I had broken into the woodwork section of Lapage street school and the police came knocking at the door, now as soon as I heard the words

"We want to speak to Harold Perkins"

I was down the cellar steps and up through the coal chute.

Now at the time I just wanted to get away from the police, in those days and at the age of eight or nine you didn't realise they would come back for you so for hours and hours I would wander around Bradford Moor park, when I was hungry I would go across the road and into the orchard and pinch a few apples to cure my hunger then back on the run until I was picked up by the police.

Because I was only eight or nine years old the police couldn't lock me up and it was a long way to the nearest remand home, so they used to take me home and tell my Mother to bring me down to the court at ten o'clock the next day, which was like a day out because when the court finished with me and added another year or two on to my already serving probation order, my Mother would go shopping in town then have a cup of tea and a biscuit in the cafe before catching the tram home so I used to think it was a treat.

Another time was when I broke into a garage at the back of our outside toilet it was where the Widdops stored their bikes and tools. Someone had put me up to this but I can't say who, I climbed onto the flat roof of the garage and there was a hatch that I forced off to gain access, once inside I had a good scout through all their tools and picked out what I thought would be best for the person who put me up to it in the first place, the first suspect was me and the police came round to our house to arrest me for breaking into this garage come bike shed now although I was only eight or nine years old I was on the wise side and hid the tools in the garden shed next to the garage come bike shed, so when the police came and said

"I had been seen climbing over the outside toilet roof"

To which I replied that I always played on the midden roofs. It was a game and we used to jump over the gaps between the midden roofs as it was a dare. Now this bit was true but the police searched the house but found nothing. They couldn't find the tools they were still in the garden shed. So that was another one I got away with. I was getting better.

Another little scam was when the fairground came round and they used to have these slot machine arcades with about twenty slot machines in and they took a penny piece. At our local fairground when it came it would have four or five of these slot machine arcades with about twenty machines in each one and an attendant to look after them. He would empty them if they got too full or fix them if they got jammed up.

My little trick was to go into the arcade and pick a machine away from the attendant and pretend I was playing it, then I would bang it with my hand, after a couple of bangs the attendant would come over and ask what was wrong and I would say "I have two pennies in this machine and it's not working" with this he would open the machine up and have a look inside to see if it was blocked up (it never was) he would shake his head stick his hand in the box where the pennies dropped and give me two pennies. As soon as I got the two pennies and his back was turned I was off to the next arcade to do the same again and by the time I had done four or five arcades it was a nice little earner. I did that for a few years before I was rumbled but at least while it lasted it was a good earner for an eight/nine year old.

I've always prided myself on the fact that if someone asked my opinion, regardless of the outcome within reason I would tell them the truth. My first holiday was when I was about eleven or twelve and my Auntie Emma and Uncle John and cousin Grace used to go to Tynemouth for a week, now whether it was one of my Mothers ploys to get rid of me for a week I don't know but she asked my Auntie Emma if they would take me with them, they said yes providing I behaved myself and didn't swear. So off we went up to Whitley Bay, Tynemouth, the lodgings were two attic bedrooms with a large bowl and a jug of cold water to get washed in. There was a bathroom which was two floors down but you wasn't allowed to get washed in it, it was only for doing other things. So Auntie Emma and Grace in one attic and me and Uncle John in a double bed in the other. Uncle John got out of bed first and put some water in the bowl and washed his face, there wasn't anywhere to empty the dirty water into only the bathroom two floors down so I had to use the same water as Uncle John after my wash in the dirty water we all went down for breakfast, we all sat at a big table and there was a lot more guests in the breakfast room I assumed they were richer than us because they were not sleeping in the attic. We were all chomping away at our breakfast when my Auntie Emma said

"Do you like this Harold"

to which I replied

"Yes thank you"

then Auntie Emma asked if I had a good night's sleep and when I replied "No" she asked me why not, I told her the truth and said I couldn't sleep for Uncle John snoring and farting, to which brought a deadly silence in the breakfast room apart from a few who gave a chuckle

"That wasn't very nice Harold"

said Auntie Emma, now I thought she meant it couldn't have been nice for me sleeping with Uncle John when he was snoring and farting, not it wasn't very nice for me to tell everyone that my Uncle John snores and farts, so I said

"No it wasn't very nice can I sleep in my own bed?"

now I didn't see what was so funny about this but all the people in the breakfast room did and had a chuckle, needless to say I got the cold shoulder all day and no spending money, so much for telling the truth.

As well as climbing down cellar grates when people had locked themselves out and running errands to make a few coppers, another little scam I had when i was about eight or nine years old was a good earner for an eight year old and it involved telephone boxes. Now in the fifties it cost about three old pennies to make a phone call, you would dial your number when the person at the other end answered the phone you would press button 'A' and your money went into the box then you could talk to the person you had rung up, if nobody answered the phone at the other end you pressed button 'B' and you would get your money back, now little old Harold Perkins used to stuff a little sponge up the slot where your pennies came down when you pressed button 'B' to get your money back when no one answered at the other end. The little sponge stopped the pennies from dropping to the bottom of the slot and wasn't released until little Harold came along and pulled the sponge out and depending on how many people had pressed button 'B' depended on how much profit I made. I had about six or seven phone boxes on my round so I made a few pennies and I always took the pennies to the post office to buy some sixpenny saving stamps with them, always using a different post office so they wouldn't get suspicious of an eight year old going in with all these pennies.

I was just finishing my last phone box and with a couple of pockets full of pennies that were weighing me down I saw a policeman who must have thought I was suspicious because he shouted at me to stop. Now I thought if he finds all these pennies on me I'm in trouble so I set off running towards Thornbury school with the weight of the pennies gangling against my legs and the fact that the policeman had longer legs than me he was catching me up so I climbed over the school gate and shot up a drainpipe and onto the roof now he may have been a faster runner than me but he was no match for little old HP climbing drainpipes and over roofs and by the time he got the caretaker with a ladder I was down the other side of the roof and away down the road with the pennies still gangling in my pockets.

It was about this time when one of my favourite hobby's was making spanish water, what I did was to get an empty sauce bottle and fill it with hot water then I would chop a half penny stick of spanish up into small pieces and put them in a jar and shake the jar for ten minutes, this produced a black tasty juice and when it had cooled down it would quench my thirst for half a day. One time I made my spanish water and was being chased up the school yard by the caretaker, my way out was the midden (a small outhouse with a flat stone roof) at the top of the yard, now the sauce bottle was hindering me to climb onto the midden so I threw the bottle onto the midden roof then jumped up to grab the edge of the stone flag so I could pull myself up onto the roof, unbeknown to me the sauce bottle had broken and when I grabbed the stone flag to pull myself up the broken sauce bottle ended up in my finger, it wasn't until I had jumped down the other side and escaped the caretakers broom handle that he had prodded me with that I realised how bad my finger had been cut, the gash went from my finger nail to the bottom of my finger and it was a very deep cut, with a makeshift bandage wrapped round my finger my Mother took me to the doctors, it was a bank holiday and there was no surgery but my Mother banged on the door of the house until the doctor came out and he wasn't happy. He glared at me and said

"Come in"

he looked at my finger and started to bandage it

"Doesn't it need stitches in it"

my Mother asked

"No it will soon heal up"

It did eventually heal up but I was left with a scar the length of my finger and because it wasn't stitched the skin didn't knit together properly so every time I got the cane at school and the cane caught my scar it would split open and bleed, needless to say this didn't stop the teachers caning me.

Living on Ravenscliffe on was no different to living at Bradford Moor the only difference was by this time in the fifty's food and clothes had come off ration and you didn't need your coupons to buy a pound of sugar or half a pound of margarine, but that never bothered us, if you didn't have it or couldn't afford it you stole it so nothing changed. When I used to walk on the railway line to the coal yard to fill the kit bag and the knapsack with coal I noticed some allotments on the other side to the cricket club and thought that's the place to go for the potatoes and cabbage for Sunday dinner. Then one Saturday night when I was helping Mum to balance her budget by pulling the spuds and the cabbage up I noticed a greenhouse that was full of grapes so I took a couple of bunches home with the spuds and cabbage, now I had never tasted a grape before and I wasn't over keen, a few weeks later I went to the picture house and saw six men and women on the screen and they were treading grapes in a big wooden vat to make wine, now I thought this could be a nice little earner, I can get the grapes all I have to do is tread them, so the next night off I went for the grapes filling the kit bag and knapsack jam full (I did give them a good shaking to get the coal dust out and line them with newspaper) at the time my Mother was working the evening shift at the local mill and didn't finish until nine thirty pm and Alfred May was out, so I had the house to myself, now I didn't have a wooden vat but mum did have a really big baking bowl it must have been two and a half feet wide and two foot deep so into the bowl went the grapes, I was just about to wash my feet when I spotted a posser now a posser was a thing they used when they were washing clothes, they would put the clothes in a washing tub full of hot water and soap flakes then grab the posser it had a copper head with holes in it and a long wooden handle like a brush handle and you would press the posser down in the washing tub and it would move the clothes about, so I thought this will save me washing my feet as I had only washed them two weeks ago. Off I set with the posser squelching and squashing the grapes, although the baking bowl was very big I had enough grapes to fill it again and thought I would get at least ten or twelve bottles of wine out off all the grapes, after about ten minutes of possing and squashing I dragged the baking bowl over to the doorway where there was a step, I thought if I get one of the big pans mum uses for cooking the spuds in and put it on the bottom of the step I can tip the baking bowl up and all the wine will go into the pan and then I can pour that in to the big bucket then fill the pan up again and so on.

Wrong when I tipped the bowl up I got a cup full of wine out of all the grapes and it tasted awful so that was my wine making scam down the pan, the grapes that were left I gave some to the lads and the family ate the rest.

I can remember when it was Whitsunday and my mates had new clothes on, in those days it was the normal thing to buy your kids new clothes and on Whitsunday walk them through the park to show them off, but not my mum she couldn't afford new clothes so it was a matter of waiting un till Mr.Donnely came with his rag cart and sort through the rags to find something that was new to me, if it was a pair of short trousers and a jumper she would wash them, iron the trousers and give me a good scrub and to keep my hair in place she would put a lump of lard in the palm of her hand hold it near the fire until it had melted then plaster it on my hair so when it was cold and set it stopped my hair from blowing about and it was cheaper than brylcreem.

An old lady lived in our yard. Her name was Mary Ellen, and she couldn't get to the shops herself. So I used to run her errands. At the time if you bought a packet of Brooke Bond tea there was a stamp fastened to the front of the packet that had a value of one farthing (four farthings to one old penny). I used to save them and, when I had filled the card with twenty-four stamps, I would take it to Driver's the grocer's and collect a sixpenny piece.

The way I used to get my stamps was this. If any of my errand customers wanted Typhoo tea or something else, because they didn't give stamps with their tea I would buy Brooke Bond, take the stamp off, and tell them they had sold out of Typhoo tea. So I had got them Brooke Bond instead.

I can remember once coming back from shopping for Mary Ellen to find, in her house, the local priest from St Mary's church and two nuns who used to come round every week begging for money or something they could sell. Most of the people who lived in our yard (about twenty) were scared stiff of this priest and his two nuns, and always gave them money.

This time Mary Ellen said, 'I'm sorry, Father, I haven't any money at all.' She opened her purse to show him that it was empty. The two nuns checked the purse to make sure it was empty. As they were looking into the purse the priest picked up one of the two silver candlesticks that Mary Ellen had on the mantel shelf. 'I may be able to get something for these if you would like to make a contribution to St Mary's Church Fund,' said the priest. Now, Mary Ellen dared not say he could not have them, so the priest picked them both up and gave one to each of the nuns to carry. All this time I was stood at the back of the house thinking they were bigger thieves than me. When they had gone I put the shopping bag on the table and gave Mary Ellen her change from the shopping bill. I wasn't going to give her it while they were there as I knew they would have taken it. Mary Ellen knew this was why I had stood at the back of the room. All of a sudden Mary Ellen started crying. It appeared that the candle sticks had been a present from her mother and she treasured them. I told Mary Ellen to keep her door locked the week after and the week after that and not to answer the door to the robbing bastards.

When I had run all my errands and I amassed my money from all my other little scams, I thought I would have a count up and then go up to the post office at the corner of Barkerend Road and Killinghall Road, next to Thompson's greengrocer's, and buy as many sixpenny saving stamps as I could afford without leaving myself short for a packet of Woodbines.

One time I had filled my savings book up with sixty sixpenny saving stamps, which meant I had one pound and ten shillings (one pound fifty today). It was a fortune for a young kid in those days, all earned by running errands, climbing down cellar grates and a few other things. I was admiring my savings book when a certain person said to me, 'I'll look after that for you so you don't lose it.' I never saw my thirty shillings savings again. Was I ever going to learn?

One more scam I used to get up to was accessing the grocer's via the beer drop. I was passing one Wednesday afternoon and saw the guy and his wife who ran the shop setting off in their car. This was not unusual, as Wednesday was half-day closing and it was a regular thing for them to go out while the shop was closed. What I did find unusual when I was passing the shop on the way back was that they were getting a delivery of beer. The wagon pulled up next to the beer drop. This was a big wooden hinged cover that pulled up to reveal a slope to slide the crates of beer down. A set of steps gave access to the cellar to bring the empty crates back up. I thought, What a stupid time to deliver crates of beer when they are out and the beer drop will be locked from inside.

I hung about to see what they would do. Lo and behold they just lifted the beer drop up. It had been left unlocked from the inside so they could have their beer delivered while they were out. Not to miss a chance like this I kept an eye on them from a distance. Sure enough, when they had finished they lowered the beer drop back into place and off they went. Convinced it was unlocked, I casually strolled across the road, looked in the window until no one was around, then lifted the beer drop up – yes, it was open. It was too much to ask a ten-year-old little Harold Perkins to close the beer drop and walk away. Down I went into the cellar. All that was down there was a few crates of beer – not much use to a ten-year-old. It would be another four years before I started drinking. So I ignored the booze and crept up the cellar steps. The door at the top was open and this led straight into the shop. To me it was Aladdin's Cave. I could have anything I wanted and didn't have to pay. But I will always remember what our Tommy had told me: never take too much; if you do it will be noticed. So I just helped myself to a few packets of cigarettes. Capstan Medium. At the time they were dearer than the ones I smoked, 'Willie Woodbines', but seeing as I was not paying I thought I would have the best. I looked in the till and found about three pound ten shillings, so I took five shillings out, helped myself to a bar of chocolate and some sweets, then let myself out of the kitchen door at the back. It was on a Yale lock so I could just pull the door closed and it would lock itself. Off I went pleased as punch with my Capstan Mediums, a bar of chocolate and five bob in my pocket. This became a regular thing to do on a Wednesday afternoon. It kept me out of mischief.

We were in Bradford Moor Park one Sunday afternoon. Keith Stocks and I had been climbing the trees and waiting for the tennis balls to get knocked over the fence of the tennis court. Then we would run off with the balls. A near-new ball could fetch nearly sixpence – it was a good earner. We had gone down to the bottom end of the park. At the side of the park ranger's house were the flower gardens, the toilets and the greenhouses. Only the park gardeners were allowed in, and a big notice on the gate told you so. Now, if anywhere had a notice that said 'Keep Out' or

'No Public Access' or 'Private No Entry', this meant we had to go in.

We climbed over the gate to where the greenhouses were, but there was nothing worth taking, so we climbed back over and I went to the toilet. On my way out a man said to me, 'Do you like birds?' I said, 'Yes,' and he said, 'There's one in that toilet that can't fly. Would you help me with it?' I was just about to go into the toilet with this man when Keith Stocks shouted, 'Harold, don't go in there!' I always had a lot of respect for Keith and looked up to him, so I did as I was told and didn't go in the toilet. It wasn't until Keith explained to me what the guy would do to me that I realised he was right and knew more than me.

This was the morning that I had broken into the woodwork section at Lapage Street School with our Tommy. As I walked out of the park, our Tommy came running up and said, 'The police are looking for us – run!' I ran back into the park and climbed over the wall at the side of the park ranger's house. Our Tommy had run to hide in the flowerbeds, but the police spotted him straight away. While they were talking to our Tommy, I was over the park wall and under this Wolsley car parked on the main road. I thought they would never find me there.

Five minutes later I could hear someone getting into the car and the doors slam shut. I heard voices and one of them was our Tommy's. I was hiding under the police car. I could hear one of the policemen saying that the caretaker from Lapage Street School had seen us both and knew us and who we were. Then I heard our Tommy saying that it was me and not him who had broken into the woodwork section. I just lay there wondering what to do next. Then I heard the car start up and away it went, leaving me face down on the road about two feet from the pavement and everyone looking at me wondering why I was there.

I always used to look forward to Saturdays as, after I had done my errands, I would go into the centre of Bradford with Keith Stocks on our shoplifting spree. We always walked into the centre, about two miles, and always got into some mischief on the way into town. We would call at the shop down Barkerend Road, the one where our Tommy used to hold the bell up to stop it tinkling so he could nick some Du Maurier cigarettes. Well, Keith and I used to do the same trick so that we had some posh cigs to smoke on our way to town. We would always go down the backs of the house on our way to town as this was where the milkman delivered, to the back door. If anyone was working in a shop or a job where they had to work all day on a Saturday and the milkman delivered after they had gone to work, the milk would still be on the doorstep. Well, it would be until Keith and I got there. We would stop at the back of St Clement's church for a smoke and a bottle of milk.

At the back of St Clements were some allotments and hen runs. After we had drunk the milk and had a smoke we would climb under or over the fence and into the hen hut to relieve the hens of some of their newly laid eggs. We always used to take the brown ones – why, I'll never know. We would hide the eggs in the long grass and pick them up on the way back from town. The reason we used to go in the hen hut on the way down to town was that if there were no eggs we could check on the way back. By doing it that way we could beat the owner to his eggs.

Next stop on the way to town was the Pops Library – this was a shop that was packed with everything from sweets, chewing gum, whistles, fire-eating tricks, you name it and they had it. It was packed full with so much gear it was a shoplifter's dream, and Keith and I called there every time we went into Bradford centre. You could spend fifteen or twenty minutes looking at all the different tricks they had on show, and it was a very busy shop. This made it easier to help yourself to some of the goods.

One time I lifted a fire-breathing pack and when I got outside I thought I would try it out. It was a small bottle of something like metholated spirits, with the instructions to put this in your mouth, take a deep breath, light a match, hold it six inches away from your mouth then breath out. So I did this. Sure enough the match lit the fumes from the metholated spirits and looked spectacular. But I should have read the rest of the instructions that said, 'On no account should you breathe in while the flame is still lit.' Little Harold Perkins did, and the flame came back and into my mouth. I suppose it was my own fault for not paying for it or reading the instructions.

Once we were in the town centre we would head for Woolworth's. Now, in Woolworth's was a toy counter and part of it was full of cap guns, the ones you put a roll of caps in. When you pulled the trigger the hammer on the gun would hit a cap and make a sound like a real gun. They were expensive, and even if they hadn't have been we still wouldn't have paid for them. The trick was we always had lumber jackets on that had a wide elastic belt at waist level. We would open the middle two buttons on our lumber jackets and pick the gun up that was in its box. With the box very close to my chest I would pull the gun out of the box, look at it, then slip it inside my jacket pocket, but make it look as if I was putting it back in the box. Then I'd close the flap on the box, put the empty box under the ones with guns in, in the middle of the pile, and casually walk out. Never run or walk quickly – you had to be two steps ahead of the store detectives.

So we had our guns. Next was Kirkgate market to get some caps. The stall where the caps were was next to the toilets. The stall keeper knew us. As soon as we appeared in the market, he never left his stall and kept an eye on us. This one was going to be difficult. The caps were piled up at the front of the stall and easy to get at, but we were being watched. Keith had the idea of causing a diversion. He said he would run down the aisle where the stall was, waving his gun about and pretending to shoot at things, going 'Bang! Bang!' When he got to the stall he would stumble and knock the pile of caps on to the floor and pretend he had hurt himself. Meanwhile I would be round the corner, and as soon as he stumbled I would run out, snaffle a handful of boxes of caps and vanish. It worked the first time but the next time the stall holder was too smart for us. He collared both of us and called the police. After getting a telling off and promising not to do it again, we were sent home.

It was always very busy in Bradford on a Saturday afternoon. Although I was ten years old I was very small for my age, probably the size of a seven-year-old. If the store detectives saw two lads walking through the store on their own they had their suspicions. One of my dodges was to look for a woman with a couple of kids and tag along with them at a safe distance so that she wouldn't be suspicious, while to anyone else it looked as though I was part of the family. If she stopped at a stall that I could nick off, nobody would be watching me. Not only did you have to use your nimble fingers, you had to use your brains as well.

On the way back from Bradford we would call at the back of St Clement's church and retrieve the eggs we had hidden in the long grass. We would take them home telling Mother that we had just been walking past the allotments and had seen these eggs in the long grass – did she want them? She knew where they had come from but never said a thing.

Our next stop depended on the time. It was old man Holdroyd's wagon. This guy lived on the green and had a greengrocer's on Barkerend Road. On a Saturday, while his wife and daughter looked after the shop, he had a mobile greengrocer's. When he had finished his rounds he would put his wagon in his garage which was at the bottom of the garden of the coalman, Sam Wynn. We used to climb over into the next-door garden, where you could pull off a window frame at the side of the garage that had just been wedged in with some plywood over it to keep the bad weather out. Once we had pulled this off, it was quite easy to gain access to the garage and therefore to the wagon. It was full of apples, oranges, pears, cabbages, lettuce – everything you could buy in a greengrocer's. We would help ourselves to as much as we could get inside our lumber jackets. It was always harder climbing back out of the window than it was climbing in, as we were fatter.

I arrived home one Saturday after a trip to Bradford centre to be met by my mother, who gave me a good hiding. One of the neighbours had seen me shoplifting and had told my mother. I got a few belts. I thought, Charming, it's OK for me to go milking petrol and breaking into garages to steal tools for her boyfriend, but not for myself.

When the school holidays came I would help the cobbler who had a shop on the corner of our block. They called him Bill Brent. He ran one of four shops owned by a guy called Willy Matthews, who said I could help Bill Brent for a week and he would pay me. I was expecting to get a full week's wage for a full week's work. I was wrong. I worked five and a half days and was expecting at least one pound. All he gave me was two shillings – the tight git. I had been working for the cobbler part time after I had finished school for the last twelve months so I was quite experienced in the shoe trade. I could strip the soles and heels of a pair of shoes and prepare them for a repair quickly and well.

I stopped going to that shop and went to another down Amberley street where a guy called Colin Knight worked. He was the guy who got me into boxing as he was an amateur boxer himself and very dedicated.

When I transferred from Tyersal School to Lapage Street School my life was made hell by some of the teachers. They knew it was me who had broken into their woodwork shop and they were going to make me suffer. Any little thing I did wrong I was caned for – not just one or two across the palm of my hand: it was six of the best. Sometimes the Headmaster would parade you on the stage at assembly time and give you six of the best in front of the rest of the school. I remember one teacher in particular who seemed to have it in for me. He would stroll around the class, standing behind you to see if you were doing your work right. He always carried a piece of wood round with him, a piece measuring one and a half by one and a half by eighteen inches, and he would stand behind you tapping this piece of wood on his thigh. When it came to my turn, I knew what was going to happen. He would come up behind me and shout at me, saying I would never make a decent student in 1,000 years, then hit me over the head or my shoulders with his lump of wood. I think if my work had been 100 per cent he would still have hit me. It carried on for about three months, every week, until I complained to the Headmaster. Then it stopped.

After twelve months had passed they stopped picking on me. Although I was still getting six of the best on a regular basis I probably deserved it, as I would never toe the line.

I can remember one time at assembly. The Headmaster said, 'Tomorrow we have a new boy joining the school. His name is Malcolm Williams and I don't want anyone to talk or mix with him. He has been a very naughty boy and has just been released from approved school.' I thought, I wonder if he said the same about me when I transferred from Tyersal. The next day, when this very naughty boy arrived, at playtime I made an effort to go and talk to him. He was no different from anyone else. He had just been unfortunate to get caught.

Linton Camp

I would have been about nine years old when me and our Tommy were sent to Linton Camp near Skipton, North Yorkshire. This place was in the countryside and consisted of large wooden huts that housed evacuees, orphans and undernourished kids. Just after the Second World War there were plenty of them about and we were sent there to recuperate.

I was as fit as a butcher's dog and couldn't fathom out why I had been sent there. Then I realised. In those days the health visitor used to visit to check your hair for nits and assess general fitness. The health man who came to see us was giving my mother one and must have thought that if he got me and my brother out of the way it would make for easier access to my mother. Our Sheila had moved out to live with my father by then, so with me and Tommy in Linton Camp I suppose it gave my mother a bit more freedom.

I remember our Tommy was in dorm one and I was in dorm two. If you wet the bed you had to take your wet sheets to dorm three. I was making my bed up about 7.15 a.m. when our Tommy came in dorm two and said to me, 'Take these to dorm three for me, I have got to go see the Headmaster.' So I took the sheets to dorm three and stood in line with the bed-wetters. When I got to the front of the queue the teacher asked me my name.

'Harold Perkins, sir.'

The teacher said to me, 'What dorm do you sleep in?'

I replied, 'Dorm two, sir,' then went away.

When it came to supper time, at seven thirty you queued in a long line to collect a big mug of cocoa. At the end of the line a teacher with a clipboard said, 'Name and dorm number?'

'Harold Perkins, dorm two,' I replied.

With this he took my mug from me and said, 'Nothing for bed-wetters.'

I said I didn't wet the bed. It made no difference. I didn't get any cocoa and needless to say our Tommy had to take his own sheets back after that.

In the dining room there was a cupboard where you could keep your own jam sent in by your parents. My mum had sent me strawberry jam and it was three-quarters full. At tea time I went to get my jam out and it had gone. So I sat down at the table. The kid across from me had my jam so I took it back. He stood up and took it back. He was bigger than me and about three years older, but he was not getting my jam. I told the teacher who was on dinner duty but he didn't want to know. So I went back to the table, picked up the jam, and smashed the boy in the face with it. Before he could get back at me I was picked up by two teachers and marched off to the Headmaster's office, where I received six of the best. It was worth it.

The teachers at Linton used to encourage you to save. I had always been a good little saver when I was at home running the errands, or climbing down cellar grates when neighbours had locked themselves out, and getting money from a few little fiddles. This money always went into the post office savings in sixpenny saving stamps, so I didn't need any encouragement to save. I used to go to dorm three (I think) every week to deposit sixpence in my new bank account. You didn't get a proper bank book – it was a folded piece of cardboard. The teacher had a book and would put in your name and the amount you had deposited, then enter the amount on your folded piece of cardboard. Although I guarded this cardboard with my life, after about three months I lost it. I went to the teacher who had been taking my sixpence a week for the previous three months. I gave him my sixpence and told him I had lost my bank book. He took my sixpence and said he would give me a new bank book the next week.

Next week came and I wanted to draw my money out, so I joined the queue. When I got to the front of the queue I said, 'I would like to draw my money out, sir.'

'Bank book,' said the teacher.

I said, 'I told you last week I had lost it and you said you would give me a new one this week.'

'What's your name?' said the teacher.

'Perkins, Harold,' I said.

'Sorry, Perkins, I haven't got your name down in my book, and unless you show me your bank book you have no money here.'

I had calculated that I had saved sixpence a week for fourteen weeks – that was seven shillings, a small fortune to a lad of nine years old. I was heartbroken. I said, 'But, sir, I have saved sixpence a week for over three months.'

'Off you go, Perkins, I'm busy.'

I went outside and cried my eyes out. It was Saturday morning, and I cried for hours.

The head teacher, Mr Sturndown, saw me crying and asked me what was wrong. When I told him he took me to the dorm where the teacher was doing the banking and asked the teacher why I couldn't draw my money out. The banker said I'd never had any money in the bank and I didn't have a bank book. I just wish I could remember the teacher's name. I would get a great deal of pleasure from revealing the name of a grown man – and I use the term loosely – who robbed a nine-year-old out of seven shillings.

While in Linton Camp I had a penknife that I treasured. I always kept it extremely sharp, for cutting branches to make bows and thick twigs to make arrows, sharpened at the end to a fine point. You were not allowed such things in Linton, but my penknife was something special to me, so I kept it out of sight.

It came in handy one time when I had a big wart the size of my fingernail that had grown on the knuckle of my left hand. The word was that if you cut a wart off you would bleed to death, but I thought, I'm not going round with a wart stuck in the middle of my knuckles. So out came the knife and I sliced the wart off in one cut. My two mates at the time were aghast and could not believe that after ten minutes I had not bled to death. I can remember wrapping my 'snot rag' round it to stem the bleeding. We called them snot rags because they were pieces cut off old bed sheets. We couldn't afford hankies.

The next day it started scabbing up and within a week completely healed, with no scar. That week my street cred went up to top of the class as my two mates went round telling everyone how I had cut a wart off my hand in one slice with my penknife.

A regular thing at Linton Camp was absconding. There were kids there who loved it and there were the ones who hated it. I hated it, but never absconded.

When someone absconded or went over the wall (which was only four foot high) they usually went up Hill Bolton. This was more like a mountain than a hill. It took a fit young lad about twenty minutes to get over the wall and to the top of the hill. This used to happen at least three or four times a week and all the teachers kept their eyes peeled on Hill Bolton for anyone who was absconding. One of the teachers had a motorcycle and sidecar, and when anyone absconded up Hill Bolton he used to let them get just over halfway, then set off on his bike and sidecar up the road that led to the top. There he would wait for the absconder, who by this time was so tired after climbing the steep hill he didn't have the strength to run away. So the teacher would grab him by the collar, put him in the sidecar and take him back to the camp. I often thought, Why do they go that way where everyone can see you? Why don't they climb over the wall at the side of the road and crawl in the grass for 500 yards then up and off without being seen? They were probably not as streetwise as nine-year-old Harold Perkins.

The recreation facilities at Linton were very poor. I can remember a playground with a load of massive ex-army wagon tyres. The biggest one of all was called Big Bertha. It took two or three of you to stand it up. Then one of you got inside the tyre for the ride while the other two pushed you round the playground. There was usually a queue for Big Bertha, and the bigger you were the quicker you got on it. They had a swimming pool that had just been built, but you had to have special permission to go in it. I can remember sneaking in out of turn, but I was soon thrown out and given a telling off.

On a weekend we used to go to the river Wharfe. I can remember going over the stepping stones across the river and swimming in the river, or trying to swim. The river was something I had never seen before.

Another thing I remember about Linton Camp was the first or second day I was there. I was in class and the teacher said, 'We are all going to write a letter to your mum and dad.' I can remember thinking, Now, this will be very difficult. I knew my mother's address but not my father's. So I told the teacher, who said, 'Well, we will write to your mother.' So I got my head down to start writing 'Dear Mum,' when the teacher asked me what I was doing. When I told her I was writing to my mum, she said, 'I am going to write on the blackboard what you are going to write down and you will copy it.' So the teacher started to write, 'Darling Mother and Father [or just Mother in my case]. I hope you are in the best of health. I am in the best of health and enjoying my stay at this lovely school set in the countryside in a picturesque village called Linton. The staff and all the teachers are very nice and very helpful, nothing is too much trouble for them. I am looking out of the window as I write this letter and I can see all the different coloured flowers gently swaying with the summer breeze and all the lambs are romping in the field. It feels so good to be at Linton. We will be going for our dinner shortly and the food here is just as good as it is at home.'

I thought, Just a minute, if I write that to my mother she will think I've lost my marbles and have me certified. 'Flowers swaying in the breeze and the lambs romping in the fields?' – what a load of old cobblers. So I wrote 'Dear Mum. I don't like it here and the teacher is trying to make me say I do. She's writing a load of rubbish on the blackboard and wants me to copy what she has wrote and send it to you.' I had got this far and I could feel the teacher behind me. She had read what I had written. She gave me a slap on the back of the head, took the letter from me and screwed it up. She gave me another sheet of paper and said, 'Copy what is on the blackboard.' I thought, I'll do that to keep the peace. I won't post it. Little did I know that once I had finished it I wouldn't see it again. They posted it, and when my mother came to see me she said, 'What have they been feeding you on to write a load of rubbish like that?' I explained I had been forced to write it.

In Linton Camp you were allowed a visit once a month. Every time my mum came she would have a different bloke with her, and she would say, 'This is your new uncle.' When they called me and our Tommy's name out for our visit our Tommy would say, 'I wonder who our new uncle will be this time.'

In those days my mother could not afford things like handkerchiefs, underpants and pyjamas. We were trying to think up something to get us out of Linton

Camp. Our Tommy came up with the idea of sending a list of clothing we wanted, but every letter you wrote was vetted before they sealed it and posted it. So we would get found out. Then our Tommy said, 'Why don't we write a letter, and when they take us on a crocodile walk we will slip it into the post box.' So we wrote the letter. The next Saturday morning came the crocodile walk (probably called this because fifty kids with a teacher front and back looked like a crocodile). Off we set. We passed a few post boxes, but because we were being watched all the time we couldn't post the letter. But finally we managed it when the teacher at the back looked in a shop window and our Tommy stood cover while I popped the letter in the post box.

A week later we got a letter from Mum saying she could not afford all these clothes, so she was sending some pyjamas and we would have to make do – if we asked for any more we would have to come home. Yes, great! So in the post in the crocodile walk went a letter asking for underpants, hankies, socks, boots – anything we could think of.

Surprise, surprise, a week later my mother appeared at the camp demanding our release immediately. This was on a Wednesday. The Headmaster would not agree to let us out until Saturday, so at seven thirty Saturday morning we were given two shillings and a few coppers and told to go home. At the gate we turned right, walked into Skipton, got a bus from Skipton to Bradford, then the tram from

Bradford centre to Bradford Moor. And who should meet us off the tram but Mum and a new uncle.

This one was called Alfred May. He had been on the scene before. He was stationed at Bellvue Barracks, but came from Southall in London. He was giving my mother one on a regular basis – so much so he was living with us, and he had put my mother in the club a few years earlier, with the result of a brother called Carl May. When Alfred May came on the scene he used to send me milking petrol so he didn't have to pay for it. This consisted of putting a tube into the petrol tank and blowing down the pipe and then sucking the petrol up until you got a mouthful. Then, providing you held the end of the pipe lower than the tank you were milking, it flowed with ease. The first time I tried it, I was sucking the petrol up the pipe into my mouth, then spitting it into the petrol can. It took me about one hour to get half a gallon. With the fumes from the petrol, by the time I got home I was drunk. Eventually he showed me how to do it properly and milking petrol became a regular job, along with pinching tools from garages so he could do repairs on his car.

The Cobbler's Daughter

When I attended Bradford Moor Junior school and it came to Physical Education, those kids who didn't have their own gym shoes had to queue up for handouts of the shoes that had been worn a few hundred times by kids with mucky, sweaty feet. With having very small feet I always ended up in a pair of gym shoes that stunk to high heaven and were three sizes too big. It was always embarrassing when they used to fall off my feet because they were too big, but not quite as embarrassing as when I had to get undressed to put my gym shorts on. All the other lads had underpants on. Because my mother couldn't afford underpants for me, she always got a vest that was too long for me, pulled it down and put a safety pin in it so that it doubled as a vest and underpants. This was OK, but when you were trying to get the pin undone without anyone seeing you it was very difficult to say the least. When we were getting dressed after PT I never put the pin back in.

The house we lived in at Bradford Moor was owned by my grandmother and grandfather Perkins, whom I only saw when I took the rent down every Friday. My mother didn't get on with Grandmother Perkins for some unknown reason, and when I had to take the rent she would say to me, 'You don't go in the house. And if she offers you any sweets, you say no, as she has probably poisoned them.' So I would take the rent down, knock on the door, and Grandmother Perkins would say, 'Come in, lad.' I would say, 'No thank you, I am OK out here' – to which I would get a huff and puff and a 'please yourself'. She did give me some sweets, which I had refused a few times. One time I heard her say to Granddad Perkins, 'Strange lad is that one – he's just refused sweets.' I used to put them down the grate as I thought they contained poison, until one time I had Keith Stocks with me, and he said, 'Don't put them down the grate, I'll eat them.' So I let Keith have one of my sweets. When he didn't die of poisoning I ate the rest myself – and I remember thinking of all the sweets I had put down the grate because my mother said they had been poisoned.

I was twelve years old, and with all the dodges and tricks I had learnt from our Tommy and a few older lads I was quite capable of looking after myself. By this time I had left junior school. Although Lapage Street Senior School was a half a stone's throw from where we lived, they wouldn't let me attend their school, as I was a bad lad for breaking into their woodwork shop some years before. So I went to Tyersal Seniors.

My first day at Tyersal I had a fall-out with a guy named David Beal. We ended up fighting in the school yard near the air raid shelter. After we had been battling for ten minutes, Frankie said, 'I've had enough.' I thought, Thank God for that – I was knackered. To my amazement his best mate, called Calab Adams, grabbed hold of me and slammed me against the air raid shelter wall. 'Let's see what you can do with me.' Although he was twelve years of age he had the body of an eighteen-year-old and was as strong as a horse. He was just about to plant one on me when David Beal grabbed his arm and said, 'No, Calab, he beat me fair and square.' So David Beal saved me from a definite hiding and I have always had the utmost respect for him – a great guy – and these two blokes became my mates.

After twelve months at Tyersal, they finally accepted me at Lapage Street Seniors. Once again on my first day I was in a scuffle, with a guy called Green. By this time I was helping the local cobbler after school and all day Saturday.

While helping the cobbler I became friendly with his daughter, who was called Ann. When the cobbler and his wife went out on a Saturday night I would go over to their house. It was the first time I had seen a television. I had heard about them, but they were for the rich, so we didn't have one. Although I was twelve years old I had to be in for 7 p.m. and in bed for seven thirty, even on a Saturday night. My mother always used to say, 'Don't forget – if you are not in this house, you'll have to sleep in the bog house.' As hard and stern as my mother was, I didn't think she would make me sleep in the outside toilet in winter, so when the cobbler's daughter said, 'What time have you got to be home for?' I said, 'Any time.' All my mates could stop out until nine o'clock and for me to be home for seven o'clock I thought was unfair. So I stayed with Ann until nine o'clock. The walk home was about twenty minutes and it was dark and cold but it had been worth it – sat with Ann all evening. That's all, nothing else.

When I got home the door was locked. That was unusual in those days. Your door was open until the last person went to bed. So I knocked on the door. The curtain came to one side, and my mother looked out and saw me at the door. Although it was dark, in the middle of the yard we had a gas lamp, and the light beamed to our door. I knew she had seen me but she didn't come to the door, so I knocked again. I got no response, knocked again, and this time she spoke. 'Bog house. I told you, if you wasn't in this house by seven o'clock you sleep in the bog house.'

'But Mum, it's freezing.'

'Bog house,' said my mother.

I knew she meant it, so I walked round for half an hour, came back to the outside toilet, sat on the toilet and tried to nod off. Every time I nodded off I would fall off the seat and bang my head on the wall.

Not being the owner of a watch I had no idea of the time. All I knew was I had been in this toilet freezing for what seemed a lifetime. I thought it must be five or six in the morning, so I walked up to the post office where they had a clock on the wall. My heart sank when I saw it was only one o'clock. So back to the bog house. After falling off the toilet seat a few more times I saw the gas light was lit in the one-up one-down, so in I went. I looked at the clock. It was six o'clock. My mum said, 'Let that be a lesson to you. When I say be in here for seven o'clock I mean it, right?'

'Yes, mum.'

So, did that teach me a lesson? No! For the sake of watching the TV and sitting in front of a big coal fire with Ann and not letting on that I had to be in by seven o'clock, I carried on sleeping in the bog house. The only thing I did learn was to stay longer with Ann until her father came home about eleven o'clock, which meant I would spend a few hours less in the bog house.

Whenever I had done something wrong or lost my temper – which happened quite often because I was a redhead, or 'ginger nut' – my mother would say, 'You are just like your father, ruled by the moon.' My mother used to say that every time there was a full moon my father would go mad. This stuck with me for years, and when I used to lose my temper I would look to see if it was a full moon. When it was a full moon I would make a special effort to be extra nice to people and not lose my temper. It was probably my way of trying to prove my mother wrong.

One time I think she was right. It was a Friday night. I was about sixteen or seventeen.

On a Friday, six of us used to get the bus into the centre of Bradford for a good booze-up. The lads, all my age, used to drink pints of beer. I had tried it but, one, I didn't like the taste and, two, there was too much volume for my little mouth and small stomach so I ended up being sick. And not having time to get to the toilet, I pulled the fireguard away from the fireplace and deposited it over the paper, wood and coal that the landlord had set ready to light the fire later. It was the Sun pub up Sunbridge Road, and if the landlord is still alive I sincerely apologise to him. But that stopped me drinking pints. So I went on to Jubilee Stout and left the lads to drink the man's drink.

After we had left the Sun pub in a hurry we headed down the road and on to Tyrell Street to a pub called the Empress. Now, this was a town centre pub and it got all kinds in. It was split up into three sections. The front Empress was always frequented by gay men. The back Empress was where the rag and bone men and domino players went. And the middle Empress was where you went if you were one of the lads. Needless to say we went in the middle Empress. On this Friday night we had probably had about four drinks each before we arrived at the Empress, so by the time we had a few more drinks we were all getting a little bit fresh.

Steve Ward and I were stood at the bar together having a chinwag when I noticed some guys who were sat down at a table. One of them was pointing a finger at me. I turned round to see if anyone was behind me. There was no one, only a sketch of a sailing ship on the wall at the back. I turned round and the chap was still pointing his finger at me. So I said to Steve, 'If he points his finger at me I'm going to smack him right on the nose.' I picked my stout up to have a drink and this guy pointed his finger at me again. So I went up to his table and just smacked him straight on the nose. When his mate stood up I was just about to smack him one when he said, 'What's all this about?' I said, 'For pointing his finger and talking about me' – to which his mate said, 'I wasn't pointing at you, I was pointing at that picture of a ship that was just behind you.' Well, if a hole had appeared I would have jumped in it. I was just about to say I was sorry when someone hit me on the head with a stool and all hell broke loose. By the time I had thrown a few kicks and punches to get some space I was off down the passage just as the police came barging in. 'In the middle room, sergeant,' I said, and we were back on to Tyrell Street and away. I never did look to see if it was a full moon.

When Nelson Gets His Eye Back

My older sister was now living with my dad. Our Tommy was in borstal. He did a full three years in Feltham. We still didn't have any more room in the one-up, one-down house because I now had two more brothers that had come along. Carl, whose dad was Alfred May, and Alan, whose dad was Harry Allen, the one that kicked me down the cellar steps. And also my mother was pregnant again.

Whenever my mother got pregnant she would keep me off school to do the washing, cleaning and shopping. With the school being so close to our house, when I went out shopping I could be seen from the school. So I had to be very alert.

One particular time I had been off school about two weeks and obviously had been seen shopping. My form teacher sent a lad to our house to ask when I was going back to school. So my mother put pen to paper and wrote a note to give to the teacher. It read, 'Harold Perkins will come back to school when Nelson gets his eye back.' So I went back to school about one week later and got caned for it. When I went home and told my mother, she said, 'I'll sort him out.' The next day I was sat in class, just after nine o'clock, when in stormed my mother. Straight up to the form master's desk she went; she picked up the cane and beat him on his head and shoulders, broke the cane in half, threw it on the floor and walked out. You could have heard a pin drop. I went scarlet and didn't know what to do. After what seemed like an age the teacher said, 'Right, get your books out and get on with your work.' Nothing was said to me. What a relief – but it was the talk of the school for weeks.

My mother was a very nice and neat writer and I used to practise copying her writing, until I could imitate it exactly. This came in useful when I used to play truant from school, then write a note that had supposedly come from my mum to say, 'Please excuse Harold for not being at school yesterday as he was not feeling well.' This went on for months until one week I played truant again for a couple of days and wrote a letter: 'Please excuse Harold for being absent for two days as he has had diorrea.' The teacher said, 'Who wrote this?' I said, 'My mum.' The teacher said, 'I don't think so. Your mother is a very good speller and she would not spell diarrhoea like that.' Another six of the best – and rumbled again.

There was a time when they used to split the class up into two groups after playtime for the last lesson of the day. Half went to music – to learn to play the recorder and read music – and the other half to current affairs. Then the next week you would swap round. They always called the full register. If they called your name out and you didn't answer, someone would shout out, 'In the other class, sir.' So at afternoon playtime Freddie Hart and I would bunk off down the road and get someone to shout out, 'In the other class, sir.' This went OK until the Headmaster wanted to see me. He came into music class and shouted, 'Perkins!' The reply was, 'In the other class, sir.' So off he went to current affairs. 'Perkins!' again. 'In the other class, sir.' We had been found out again, so next morning into the Headmaster's office for another six of the best.

The following week I was put in the music class. A recorder was stuck into my mouth and a sheet of music put in front of me. Now, the rest of the class had an advantage over me: they had been attending the class every other week for ten weeks. So when we had to play part of the 'Sugar Plum Fairy' on the recorder, I sounded like a foghorn – and the music teacher, a Mr Cartwright, knew it. He pulled the recorder out of my mouth and smacked me over the head with it. With this I stood up and punched him with all my might right on the nose. Mr Cartwright was a big guy and I was only small, so he grabbed me by the scruff of the neck and dragged me to the Headmaster's office.

'Mr Walls, this boy has just punched me in the face. Give him six of the best.' Only the head teacher and the deputy head were allowed to dish out six of the best. I said that if he had not hit me over the head with the recorder I would not have punched him, so the Head said, 'I'll deal with him, Mr Cartwright, you can go back to the class.' Once I had told him my story and that all the class had seen him hit me as I was on the front row, he said to me, 'Perkins, get yourself home.' There were only two weeks left before the end of term, so he put me in current affairs and kept me out of music.

Another story I can tell about Lapage Street School concerns Mr Beam, who was the Arts and Crafts teacher. When you went into his classroom he always wrote something on top of the blackboard and would ask you what it meant or why it was different. One day he wrote 'Cadbury's' on the board with the d and the b joined, and went on to tell us that was like a trade mark. When you looked at it and saw the d and b joined without seeing any other letter you would still know it was Cadbury's.

Next time he put the word 'ambidextrous' on the board. Now, I thought this was being able to play with yourself with both hands. Mr Beam said, 'Can anyone tell me what that word means?' I thought, If you knew what it meant, you're not going to stand up in class and tell your mates it means you can play with yourself with both hands. Why would a teacher be asking something like that? And, when no one comes up with the answer, how will he explain it? Then the local brainbox put his hand up and said, 'Sir, it means you can write with both hands, or you can use your left hand as good as your right hand.' I thought, That sounds different, but you are wrong. 'Correct!' said Mr Beam. 'That's exactly what ambidextrous means.' By the way, I am not ambidextrous, and you learn something every day.

By the time I was thirteen years old, our one-up and one-down was a bit overcrowded. Alfred May was a permanent lodger, so when the coalman came it was back to one bag of coal instead of five, and I didn't have to count the sacks.

There were six of us living there: Mum, Alfred May, myself, Carl, Alan and a new sister called Susie, named after my favourite auntie, my mum's sister. So it was time to move. We were shown a rented corporation house on Ravenscliffe Estate, Bowness Avenue: three bedrooms, living room and a kitchen plus a parlour with a bay window. In those days, when you moved into a corporation house from a back-to-back, your mattresses and settee were fumigated to get rid of any bugs or fleas. I was pleased about this as I had to push all the furniture five miles on a pram on my own to the new house, and anything that went to be cleaned was picked up from the old house and delivered to the new house. I can remember thinking to myself as I was pushing the pram up Killinghall Road, loaded with a big heavy wooden wardrobe, I wish this had bugs and fleas in it – then it would have been cleaned and delivered.

After starting at 6 a.m. and getting a cup of tea at the start and end of each journey, I finally made my last trek of five or six deliveries and finished at 9 p.m. I had moved all the chairs, table, sideboard, wardrobe, beds, pots and pans, etc. And it had taken me fifteen hours. I sat down in the new house and Alfred May said, 'I'll make you a cup of tea, lad' – something he had never done. It was always Mum, or I had to make it myself. I felt great: Alfred May making me a cup of tea. I'll mention it in my letter when I write my monthly letter to our Tommy. He was still in borstal.

'We have run out of tea and sugar,' said Alfred May.

I thought it had been too good to be true. 'I will just have some milk and a slice of toast, then,' I said.

'Sorry, no bread and only a mouthful of milk.'

I knew of a small shop which was about half a mile away that would be easy to get in. So, armed with a kitbag I set off. I arrived at the shop. I entered it quite easily and started to fill the kitbag. I was looking at things I had never had before, like salmon and coffee, so I filled the kitbag full of goodies. It was so heavy I could hardly lift it. When I got back to the new house I put the bag down on the floor.

'Well done, lad, I'll make you a cup of tea,' said Alfred May.

'I think I'll have coffee,' said I, seeing as I'd never had coffee before.

So Alfred set about making me a coffee. 'You didn't get any sugar,' he said.

In my excitement at seeing the salmon and the coffee I had forgotten the sugar. So up I got, back to the shop and collected two bags of sugar. When I got back it was about one o'clock in the morning. I sat down to a cup of coffee and a salmon sandwich, the two things I had never tasted before. And I got a pat on the back from Alfred May.

So here I was on this big estate. I didn't know anybody and was going to a school (still Lapage Street) nearly five miles away. It was two bus rides, and with waiting for the connecting bus it was a one-hour journey, so I had to get up more than an hour earlier than before.

The first day on the bus I met a lad who went to Lapage and lived on Ravenscliffe. He was called Brian Delaney. We teamed up together on the school run, which made it more exciting. I found out that Brian had lived near Lapage and moved to Ravenscliffe about six month earlier, so I arranged to meet him and his gang that evening after tea. His mates were Norman Bannon, who went to Hutton School which was near to Ravenscliffe, and Carl Mendies, who went to a Catholic school. We all got on together despite me being a bit 'wider' than them. When I say that, I mean that I was brought up to steal things, they weren't. At night we would all meet in the sand pits, a disused area at the end of Ravenscliffe Avenue by Fagley Woods, and smoke our woodbines, tell a few stories and get up to mischief.

One night Carl Mendies and myself were getting bored, so I decided to do something that would give me a buzz or a thrill. I said to Carl, 'Shall we break into the Scout place?' This was part of a chapel between the shops on Ravenscliffe Avenue and it was where the Scouts had their meetings. I smashed a window to get in. Carl was on the lookout. I don't think he wanted to get involved, but I forced him into it. I climbed back out of the window with nothing, vowing never to break in there again. Carl was saying, 'Let's get out of here.' I said, 'I know where we can get some money – come with me.'

On our way through Ravenscliffe towards Greengates, Carl kept saying, 'Where are we going?' Five minutes later, I said, 'There,' and pointed my finger towards the garage that was open to sell petrol at night.

'How are we going to get money from there? There's someone there all the time. When he sees a car pull up, he comes out of his kiosk, puts petrol in the car and takes the money and goes back to his little kiosk and puts the money into the till.' At the time I carried a Webley Senior air gun in a shoulder holster. I pulled the Webley out and said, 'With this. You keep a look out and when the road's clear of traffic, give me a wave. I will go up to the guy in the kiosk, stick the gun in his back and make him empty the till. While I'm doing this, all you have to do is keep an eye out for cars coming into the garage. If you see one coming in, stop it and say, sorry we are out of petrol.'

To this, Carl said, 'No way, I'm going home.' That was the end of the Greengates garage grab.

Carl Mendies had a paper round at Poulter's newsagents in Undercliffe. I asked if they would put my name on the list for paper boys. I used to help John on his round until I got a round of my own. This consisted of delivering sixty Telegraph and Argus, a couple of Evening Post and the odd magazine. For this I was paid two shillings a week. On my way round people always used to ask me if I had any spare papers. It wasn't long before I realised I could make some extra pennies if I had more papers. So I set my little brain working overtime and came up with the idea to get some spare papers to make extra cash.

When you went into the shop to pick your papers up, they were all in delivery bags ready for you to go off on your round. We all used to count the papers to make sure we had the correct amount. If you were short, you would say, 'One paper short, Mrs Poulter,' and if they were busy they would say, 'Take one from the pile.' If they were not serving anyone then they would come and count the papers to check you weren't trying to pull a fast one.

So what I used to do was wait until they were serving and had a few customers in the shop. Then I would say, 'One short.' 'Take one from the pile,' came the reply, and with this I would take two or three, and I always sold them on the way round. Now a Telegraph and Argus at the time cost one old penny. If I could snaffle an extra eighteen to twenty papers a week I had nearly doubled my wage.

One of the things I had to do when we lived on Ravenscliffe was to keep the home fires burning. This meant carrying a kitbag and a knapsack to the coal yard via the rail track, so I wouldn't be seen easily – only a quarter of a mile away. I would get there and look for a wagon that had the flap down and was nearly empty. This allowed me to stand on the wooden deck and not on the coals, which would be noisy. I would fill the kitbag up, tie the top secure, then stand it at the opening of the carriage; same with the knapsack. I would climb down and first put the knapsack on, placing the straps over my shoulders and pulling the straps very tight. Then I would lower the kitbag down on to the back of my neck and shoulders and off I would go. The hardest part was going down the very steep railway embankment where the cricket field was. With about fifty kilos of coal on your back, it was not easy.

I don't suppose Ravenscliffe was any different from any other council estate. We had our gangs and territories and woe betide anyone who dared to come on to our territory without being invited. The punishment was being tied to a tree. We had a special tree in the woods where the rope and a can were kept.

We would tie them to the tree, all pee in the can, pour it over them, then let them go.

The Webley Senior gun that I had was a pump-action gun that fired slugs and darts. Although you had to be eighteen years old or over to buy one of these, I acquired mine with no trouble at all. Getting ammunition – that was the problem. At the sports shop you had to show your birth certificate or a note from your dad to say they were for him. So, back to the days of writing my own school notes, I used to write, 'Please would you supply for my use only 100 lead pellet slugs and ten darts, and please give them to my son for delivery. Thank you.' It always worked.

We used to have gang fights. The Otley Road mob used to come up and we would meet them at the end of Ravenscliffe estate and knock seven bells out of one another for no reason at all. One time I had a confrontation with one of the Otley Road mob, called Tony. Although I carried a gun I very rarely used it. It was just for show. I was against knives. I was having a go with this Tony when he pulled a knife on me and lunged at me with it. I wrestled it off him and stabbed him in the arm. This ended the fight and everyone went away, but not before Tony had asked for his knife back. I gave it to him with one hand, but made sure he saw my Webley in the other.

At this time I was still helping the cobbler, but only on a Saturday morning at a different shop from the one in Barkerend Road. This one was down Amberley

Street, but still near Lapage School, so I used to pop down to the shop at dinner times. Colin Knight, who ran the shop and repaired the shoes, was a great guy and I looked up to him. He'd treat me like an adult, not like a kid. He was an amateur boxer. He boxed for the YMCA and trained Monday, Wednesday and Friday nights, with a ten-mile run on Sunday morning. I didn't take a lot of talking into it and soon I was hooked on the boxing. I even gave up smoking for ten months. I used to train Monday, Wednesday and Friday for three hours a night, do the run on a Sunday morning – ten miles in hobnail boots. They were supposed to make you light on your feet when you got in the ring.

The first time I climbed into the ring to spar for three rounds of three minutes each I was put in with a lad called Kevin. He was two years younger than me. I was a south-paw (lead with your right hand) and had fought in the street but not in a ring. So when we got into a clinch and you were supposed to push each other away I thought, This is a too good a chance to miss, and I gave him a good right hook. Straightaway Mark Good, the trainer, stopped the fight, took me to the neutral corner, and said, 'While you are in this ring you fight by the rules and you do not throw a punch while in a clinch. Stay there.' With this he went over to Kevin and had a word with him. We then carried on sparring.

There was only the last round to go, the idea of sparring is to practise boxing but not throw a hard punch. I didn't know this, so in the last round this Kevin ran rings round me and gave me a hiding. I found out later that Mark Good had said to Kevin – who had been boxing since he was nine and had been a schoolboy champion – 'Teach him a lesson for giving you a right hook in the clinch.' And he did. My career in boxing lasted only ten months. They swapped me from a south-paw to orthodox, but I didn't make the grade. I was too impatient and bad-tempered to make a boxer.

One day before I had packed up the boxing I had been training at the YMCA and my mate was playing a friendly game of rugby on the playing fields at Bradford Moor. I thought I would go along and give him a little bit of support. So I went straight from the YMCA and got the bus to Bradford Moor. When I got there both teams were limbering up. My mate came over and said they were two players short in their team – would I make one up? I said no, as I had never played rugby before and I only had my boxing gear with me. After five minutes he persuaded me to join in. They gave me a shirt to wear but I had to wear my boxing shorts. Now these shorts were my pride and joy: black silk with a white stripe down each side.

My mate said because I was a good runner he would put me on the wing. So off I went running up and down the wing, not touching the ball for about ten minutes. Then all of a sudden my mate threw the ball to me and said, 'Run like hell!' I set off with the ball, running up the wing towards their touchline, when, wham! This guy from the other side stuck his elbow into my face. My feet shot off the ground and I was flat on my back with one eye closed through the blow and my beloved boxing shorts full of mud. This was just too much for me to comprehend, so I stood up and smacked the guy right on his nose. There was blood everywhere. At this the referee came running over with my mate and said I couldn't do things like that. He sent me off. I thought, He can stick his elbow in my face and that's OK, but as soon as I put my fist in his face to get my own back it isn't OK. So my rugby career lasted about fifteen minutes. I never played again.

Still at Ravenscliffe, I used to try to get out of the house when my mother and Alfred May were arguing. He used to hit her and I didn't want to get involved. But one night about 8 p.m. they started. I came down the steps and through the living room and he was hitting her. So I had a go at him and then my mother started hitting me. I thought, Charming, I'm trying to protect her and now she's hitting me. She kicked me out of the house. Unlike winter nights sleeping in the bog house, this was summer. I had to go to school the next day, so I walked over to Bradford Moor Park, spent the night in the park, went to school next day and at dinner time went to see Colin the cobbler. He said, 'You can stop with me,' which I did. I never told school I had moved as I had only a few months to go before leaving.

I was waiting to go to court on a charge of stealing a car and demolishing a bollard in Huddersfield. Until I was due in court I had to stay at the approved school in Leeds. The residents were aged from eleven to sixteen years. I kept myself to myself until the local 'daddy', as we called the bully, tried to order me about. He was bigger and older than me, and I didn't want to get into any more trouble than I was already in by having a go at him. I waited on him for a couple of days, until one Saturday afternoon when we were playing cricket and I was batting. He was on the other side and behind the stumps. After a couple of overs the bowler bowled a ball that bounced high and to my left-hand side. I swung at the ball, missed it on purpose and smacked my bat very hard in the face of the daddy. He went down and I leant over him and said, 'Don't ever pick on me again or you'll get more of that.' When the two teachers came running over I said it was an accident. He told them I did it on purpose. I got away with it and he never came near me again.

The reason I stole the car was that I had been out drinking with our Tommy and his two mates. Although I was only fourteen I looked eighteen or nineteen, so I never had any trouble getting served in a pub. I was showing off. They would be nineteen or twenty and couldn't drive. I said I could. They didn't believe me, so I took a car from the Victoria Hotel. Our Tommy's mates got in and we drove to Huddersfield, about ten miles from Bradford. I had never been to Huddersfield, so I didn't know where I was going.

Eventually the police gave chase, and we were tearing around Huddersfield at a fair pace. By this time there were three police cars on our tail. I cut down a narrow muck road and put my lights out so it would make it harder to see the car. I realised I was in the sewage works, and the narrow roads I had been going round were in fact the gaps between the sewage dams. Needless to say I lost the cops. We abandoned the car and walked over a pipeline bridge that went over the river. By this time it was about 4 a.m., so I said, 'Let's hide somewhere until all the workers are going to work, then split up and make our own way back to Bradford.' I was out-voted by the two older lads and we decided to walk back to Bradford via the main road.

We hadn't been walking long when up pulled a police car. Our Tommy's mates gave themselves up, but I ran and jumped over a wall and into the river. I swam to the banks on the right-hand side and, surprise, surprise, guess who pulled me out? Yes, the cops, who then bundled me into the back of a police car and gave me a few smacks. They took me down to the nick and played good cop, bad cop with me. One knocked me off the chair, by means of engaging his fist against the side of my face. When bad cop went out of the room, the good cop would say, 'I'm sorry about that, Harold, I don't like him. You can trust me. Now, tell me who was driving the car.' When I said, 'Me,' he sent the bad cop in to knock me off the chair again, and the bad cop said, 'No more lies, this time we want the truth.' It wasn't until another cop came in and said that the other two had confirmed I was driving that he stopped knocking me off the chair.

So for this showing-off trick I spent two weeks in approved school. When I went to court, my probation officer stood up and gave me a glowing report. He said

I had not been given a chance in life. If the judge would spare me from going to approved school and give me probation instead, he would straighten me out. It worked, and I merely got three years' probation on top of the probation that I was already doing.

The Entrepreneur

When I left school it seemed the natural thing to do: I became a cobbler on a wage of one pound seven shillings and sixpence per week. After seven months I got fed up with it. My mate Carl Mendies, who worked for an electrical engineering firm called James Tate's on East Parade, Bradford, told me there was a vacancy for an apprentice electrical engineer. I applied for the job and started on a wage of one pound ten shillings and threepence per week. Being the new boy I had to run the errands. Everyone called me the gofer – go for this, go for that. At first I wasn't keen on the gofer's job until I realised I could make a few quid on the side.

About 100 people worked at this place, and most of them dined in the works canteen. The canteen didn't do meals or sandwiches, only cups of tea. It supplied plates, to put your own food on, plus knives and forks. So if I went round and took orders for fish and chips sixty times, I would order sixty fish and forty bags of chips, and spread the forty bags of chips over sixty plates of fish, making a profit of twenty bags of chips. If they ordered a buttered teacake, which was half a pence dearer than an unbuttered one, I used to buy unbuttered and butter them myself, adding a few more bob into the coffers.

Another trick was the meat pies. Everyone liked a Munz pie from Munz butcher's shop, but these were a penny dearer than the ones at Magson's. I once tried to pass off a Magson's pie as a Munz, but Bill who worked in the pattern-makers' shop pointed out that a Munz pie had a small hole in the crust on top where they poured in the gravy, and the Magson's pies didn't. So, I thought, this is the test time. The next day I took orders for ten pie and chips and bought the Magson's pies instead of the Munz. All I did was make a hole in the crust to make it look like a Munz pie. Hey presto! It worked, and I had made an extra one penny on each pie. I was beginning to like my job.

When you took such large orders to the shop, the shopkeeper would reward you for giving them the custom, so I thought I would get the shops competing against one another. The teacake shop would give me an extra two teacakes a day, which meant I made an extra fourpence just on buying the teacakes. So I said, 'The shopkeeper up the road will give me three teacakes a day if I give him the order.' The one who gave me two upped it to four. The fish shop used to give me a free fish and chips every day, so I said, 'The fish shop up Otley Road said he will give me two fish and one portion of chips.' They agreed to an extra two fish and two portion of chips. Yes, things were getting better. I was earning more money every week, so everything was going fine.

My wage was one pound ten shillings and threepence per week, and I was making an average of four pounds a week from my little scams. I was very pleased, until George the foreman said, 'I want you to show this new lad the ropes. He will be taking over your job as gofer, and you're going on the bench.' I didn't tell the new lad about my scams. I thought, Why should I? On the bench I was now earning one pound ten shillings and threepence per week. I was not a happy lad.

I had heard that coalminers could earn good money, so I applied to the Coal Board. But before you could go down the pit you had to go on a twelve-week training course at Wakefield, first week at Newton Hill. It was a man-made pit that was just like the real thing, but only six feet below ground. This was where you did your hands-on training. The second week you spent at Wakefield Technical College, where you were taught the technical side, then back to Newton Hill for the third week, and so on.

There were about thirty of us on this course, aged between fifteen and eighteen. I would be about fifteen years of age. I first attended Newton Hill on 30 December 1957. We were split up into two teams of about fifteen in each team. The guy who looked after our team was Brian Ball, from Doncaster. He had worked down the pit for quite a few years before he took the job of training officer. After a couple of weeks he took me on one side and said, 'I am going to make you a team captain. Your job will be organising the team and telling them what to do.' I could feel my head getting bigger. Here I was, not quite sixteen, and I would be telling all the other lads what to do. I was soon to learn my first lesson in how to deal with people.

First thing of a morning I would have a meeting with Mr Ball. He would tell me what he wanted our team to do, from loading tubs with coal, tipping them, chocking the gates up with wood spars, first aid, to cleaning toilets out. There was a big guy in my team. He was about seventeen years old, six foot tall and a bully, and I didn't like him. So when it came to who should be cleaning the toilets out, guess who? Yes, the big bully. Little old Harold Perkins was going to bring this guy down to size. When I told him he was on toilet duty he refused. I said to him, 'If you don't do your stint today I'll make you do two stints and report you for disobeying orders.' I think this team captain title had gone to my head and I thought I could tell anyone what to do. I was shouting, 'Hey, don't just stand there – move!' and generally bawling, until Mr Ball took me on one side. He said to me, 'To be a good team captain you have got to find out who you can tell what to do and who to ask, because some will do the job if you ask but not if they are told. And sometimes if you ask they don't do it – then tell them.' So this was my first lesson in how to deal with people. I agreed with Mr Ball. But the big bully still had to clean the toilets out, which he did when Mr Ball told him if he didn't do what I told him to do he would be suspended from the course, which would mean he would never get down the pit.

Over the next ten weeks he used to look daggers at me, and I only put him on toilet duty another three times.

After a training period of twelve weeks I was working down Gomersal Colliery, shovelling coal out of a three-foot seam and into a tub which held about three quarters of a ton. Then I would tram it (push it) to the tippler a mile from the face, starting at 6 a.m. and finishing at 2 p.m. with just one half-hour break for a 'snap' (a miners' expression for a snack). It was hard work but I enjoyed it and the wage, six pounds seven shillings and sixpence per week, was very good. This job came to an end when I was working in water for a week, soaked through all day long and I became poorly. I got my doctor's note and sent it in to get my sick pay, but I did not know I had to send it to the Coal Board first. When I went back to work three weeks later, I got the sack. Another road had come to an end.

My next job was as a flour boy. This was working for a local bakery. The flour boys had to unload the wagons that brought the sacks of flour. The sacks weighed 120 lb and were ferried to the flour rooms by a conveyor. Then they were stacked two high on a barrow and pushed to wherever the foreman indicated. If they were stacked three high, you had to carry the 120 lb sack on your shoulder and run round and stack it on top of the two high ones. Hard work – but the wage of five pounds and ten shillings was not bad, and we had some good times. The foreman was Michael Blackey, an ex-commando who was trained in unarmed combat. At lunchtime occasionally he would challenge four of us to tackle him. This always took place on top of the flour sacks, where it was a soft landing. Thank God, because we never got the better of him.

Eventually I got to be head flour lad and was in charge of the bonus scheme. You could earn a bonus of two shillings and sixpence, five shillings or seven shillings and sixpence (three half crowns as it was then). I always got the three half crowns, being the head lad. All my mates got two or three half crowns. It seemed a fair way of doing it. On a Friday afternoon you changed your overalls and Michael the foreman used to go down and see one of the managers. You could set your clock by him. He would go down the steps at 3 p.m. and be back up at three thirty.

When a new lad asked how he could get three half crowns bonus, I thought we would have some fun. I told him he would have to go into Michael Blackey's office and drop his pants at exactly three twenty-five. In goes the new lad, drops his pants, bends over the desk and in comes Michael. Well, all hell was let loose. Michael went barmy. Although I denied setting it up, he said if anything like that happened again he would sack me. He was a nice guy and fair.

Before this we had stripped a lad naked and tied him to the conveyor belt. When the confectionery girls went up to the canteen (the canteen steps ran at the side of the conveyor) we set the conveyor going and stopped it where he was in full view of the girls.

Another prank was sending the new lads down to James Sheen's office on a Friday for some soap flakes to wash the overalls. At that time there was no such thing. We did get a telling off, but were never threatened with the sack and I was still head flour lad with a bonus of three half crowns.

Although I liked the flour gang I got itchy feet and had the idea of setting up my own window-cleaning round. So I left the flour gang and went round an estate knocking on doors asking if they wanted their windows cleaned. When I had canvassed what I thought would keep me going for about three days I bought some ladders, a bucket, leather and a scrim (this polished the windows, or so I'd been told) and set off on my round. I was self-employed and had to put my self-employed stamp on every week, which I did. I think this was about one shilling and eleven pence and, I thought, not bad for a seventeen-year-old. I've got my own business. I was now earning eleven pounds a week. It was like being a millionaire.

All these things you hear about window cleaners, and what they see and do, I think are greatly exaggerated. I only ever got propositioned once, and she must have been forty; with me being seventeen it was a big gap. As soon as I put my ladders up to her windows she would come out and put some clean water in the bucket. When I was cleaning the upstairs windows she would be prancing round each bedroom with very little on. When I had finished her windows she always made a cup of tea for me and I would sit in the house supping tea and eating her biscuits, while she sat on the sofa showing me her stocking tops. This happened every two weeks and I never had more than tea and biscuits. So I was earning a few quid and enjoying life.

Then a guy I worked with on the flour gang who was out of work asked if he could give me a hand, so I bought some more work from another window cleaner and set him on. Everything went well, until our Tommy had a bit of trouble at home and said he wanted to get away for a few weeks. I left this so-called mate to run my business and said he could have everything he earned. Me and our Tommy went down to the railway station. Not knowing where to go, I went to the ticket office and said, 'Where is the next train going to?'

'Birmingham New Street,' was the reply.

So off we went, and ended up in Birmingham. After five weeks, money was getting thin and our Tommy was getting homesick, so off we went back to Bradford. I thought, I'll clean a few windows to get a few bob, and went to the house where I stored my ladders in their yard, put the ladder up, knocked on the door for some water, and the lady said, 'I thought you had sold out, because two new men came a few days ago and said they were the new window cleaners.' When it all came out, this so-called friend whom I had trusted with my business had sold it off and done a runner with the money.

The Jail Bird

I went down to the labour exchange looking for a job. 'Got a vacancy here for a labourer at a scaffolding company,' said the man behind the counter. I thought, This could be exciting, climbing up church steeples and swinging about hundreds of feet up. Yes!

So off I went to Mills Scaffold Company Ltd, Stanley Road, Bradford. The guy who interviewed me was Matt Dixon, a Geordie. He was the guy who hired and fired. He took one look at me and said, 'You are not big enough to be a scaffolder.' Looking out of the window at some men loading a wagon, he said, 'That's how big you should be if you want to be a scaffold erector.'

I looked out and saw two men about six-foot-three tall and built like brick outhouses. I thought, I'm not having this, and said, 'Anything they can do, I can do. The only thing I can't do is reach as high.' To my surprise he said, 'Right, we will give you a trial.' I was sent to a building site in Leeds to start my career as a scaffold erector.

My first day consisted of carrying five-foot, six-foot and seven-foot tubes up an eight-storey block of flats. With two flights of steps to each floor and seven steps to each flight, that was 112 steps up and 112 down, all day long, week in, week out. I thought, Thank God they only go to ten storeys.

Anyone new who started was put with me. Some lasted two days, some one day, and some only a few hours. One guy said to me, 'How long have you been doing this?' When I told him five weeks he said, 'You must be wrong in your head,' and walked off. He had only done a couple of hours. I was beginning to think, Am I right in my head? What kept me going was the voice of Matt Dixon saying, 'That's how big you've got to be to be a scaffold erector.' I thought, They are not getting the better of me – probably the same as a wild horse thinks when he's being broken in. So I soldiered on.

I was on two shillings and ten pence halfpenny an hour. We used to get paid ten hours a day, and work over at night plus all day Saturday and Sunday, so I was on a good screw and could afford to buy an expensive suit and some nice shoes – something I never had when I was a kid. So instead of boozing all my wages away with the rest of the scaffolders I spent my money on good clothes.

I can remember the first suit I had tailor-made. I paid eleven pounds for the cloth and twenty guineas to have it made up. That was in 1960. When I went out I felt like the bee's knees. Because I didn't mix and go boozing with the other employees, the foreman on the site, Peter Atkinson (or 'Ako' as everyone called him), gave me the nickname of 'Maverick'. It was not because I looked like Brett or Bo Maverick from the TV series. He said it was because I was a 'lone steer'. I went to the library and looked up 'maverick'. Sure enough, it was a lone steer, and the name stuck with me.

The first works do I went to was a pre-Christmas event at the Cricketers at Baildon Green, Baildon. All the scaffolders would meet and reminisce about jobs they had done in the past. I had worked at Mills Scaffold for about six months. All that time I was on a site in Leeds, so I never went to the yard in Bradford where you met all the other scaffolders. Although I had been there six months I didn't know many of the others. When word got round that 'Maverick' would be at the Christmas do, everyone was waiting to see what this new guy looked like. What a disappointment they all got – they were thinking a big six-foot six-inch good-looking bloke with a head full of black hair. What they saw was a small ugly lad with hardly any hair. I would have been about eighteen.

I had been working at Mills Scaffold Ltd for about seven months. Very hard work, but I enjoyed it. A so-called friend said he was in debt, and if he didn't raise

£340 by Tuesday they would come and take all his belongings away. Could I lend him any money? I didn't have thirty-four pounds let alone three hundred and forty, so I told him no. He said, 'Can't you do what you used to before?' I said, 'No, that's all behind me. I've got a good job and I'm not going back to that life of robbing. After a lot of begging and tears from his wife I gave in and said, 'I'll do it once to help you out, but don't ask again'.

Off I went to rob a few shops and pubs to get him a few quid to pay his debts off. I always used to do shops or pubs, never anyone's home. I always thought, and it is a fact, that if you screwed a pub and got £200 the landlord would tell the insurance that £900 had gone missing. I made them easy money, so I didn't feel guilty. Here I was with a good job, been going straight for two years, and I was going back to the bad life for someone else. I must have been mad. I got him the £340 and got caught and sentenced to borstal for nine months to three years. What a fool I had been. But I had done the crime, now I would do the time. It was no good crying over it, and that's how I thought about it.

My first taste of prison was Armley jail in Leeds, a grim, dismal place. I think I went into Armley on 27 December 1960 and was in a cell on my own, which I preferred. Most of the time you were one'd up or three'd up for obvious reasons – very rarely two'd up. The cell I was in had a tiny window with half the glass missing. On a cold December night with the wind blowing it was freezing, so I slept fully clothed. I spent about a month in Armley and soon got educated a little bit more.

From Armley I was shipped down to Latchmere House via Pentonville and Wormwood Scrubs. The way they transported you was to handcuff you to another inmate, put you on the prison bus and take you to Leeds railway station where you boarded the train for London. Most of the inmates were young lads, or 'YP's as we were referred to. I was expecting to be cuffed to another YP, but they cuffed me to this big guy who was about thirty. I found out he was doing fourteen years for bank robbery and was being taken to London to appear in court on 'production' – another term for being found guilty for another crime before you were tried. Now, when you are cuffed to someone you get very close. The only time the cuffs come off is when you are going to the toilet, and then one of you is cuffed to something or someone and the other is cuffed to a screw who escorts him to the toilet and back, then cuffs him back on to you. This gangster confided in me and said he was expecting another seven years on top of his fourteen years he was doing, and he was looking to do a runner. He told me that if I did a runner with him he would look after me, give me a job in his gang, and I would have a new name and birth certificate.

Now, the most I would be doing would be three years, and all I wanted was to do my time and get back to scaffolding. I didn't want to be on the run and looking over my shoulder every minute. So I said no thanks, but he kept insisting, as without my co-operation he wouldn't get far being handcuffed to me. He told me he had a car waiting outside of the station, next to the prison bus that was transporting me to Latchmere House and him to Pentonville. Sure enough, when we got off the train and walked up the platform to where the prison bus was, there was a car with the driver at the wheel and a guy ready to open the back door for a quick get away. I could feel the butterflies in my stomach. We walked up the platform. When we got about fifty feet away from the prison bus, he said, 'When I say "now", run with me,' to which I spluttered a very nervous, 'No.' He scowled at me all the way to Pentonville and had a few choice words for me as he stepped off the bus. I have never been as pleased to be handcuffed to the bus rail as when they released his cuff from me, and I was equally glad to arrive at Latchmere House via the Scrubs.

Latchmere House was where you were assessed to see which borstal they would send you to. If you were the quiet type you would be shipped off to an open borstal, like Wetherby or Hatfield. If you were a hard man you would be sent to Portsmouth, or 'Pompey', as it was known. And if you were an obstinate, 'I'm against anyone in authority' type, they sent you to Feltham. I was somewhere between Portsmouth and Feltham. I had a chip on my shoulder and I couldn't see it, but a guy I worked with in the gym at Latchmere House could see it. The day before I had to see the psychiatrists, everyone saw this man. He was the one who decided which borstal you went to. They called him Tarney. He was a scouser, I think his name was John, and if he his still about I thank him for the advice he gave me. He said, 'When you go to see the psycho, take that chip off your shoulder and put an act on. Tell him you had a bad upbringing and you regret what you have done. Really lay it on, and if you can cry that should do the trick. You will go to an open borstal and you'll have more chance of getting out early. If you carry on as you do you'll end up in a closed borstal, and you'll do the full three years.' In a closed borstal you were locked in, whereas in an open one you could virtually walk out at any time. I think if on the day I saw the psycho they had been giving Oscars out, I would definitely have got one. I really laid it on and was shipped up to Hatfield, near Doncaster. Thanks once again to Mr Tarney from Liverpool.

I kept my nose clean while I was at Latchmere House and got a good job in the gym. There were lads there who couldn't see beyond the ends of their noses. If you got into trouble or were disrespectful to one of the screws, you were punished for a maximum of three days. One of the punishments was shovelling coal, but this was a little bit different. There were two tons of coal at one side of the parade ground, which you had to get to the other side of the parade ground, and this is how they made you do it. First of all you would salute the screw, who kept his beady eye on you; then you would ram the shovel into the pile of coal, then hold the shovelful of coal at shoulder height. Then you had to march at the double, lifting your knees up as far as they would go up to your chest. You would march like this at the double to the other side of the parade ground, deposit your shovelful of coal (or what was left of it) on the ground, salute and say 'sir' to the screw, then march at the double, lifting the knees up again, back to the pile of coal. You would salute and say 'sir' to the screw, in with the shovel and off you went – doing that all day long. When you got to the last shovelful and picked up all the bits of coal you had dropped while you were 'knees up at the double', you just started again and transported the two tons of coal back to where you had just brought it. Now, I never had to do that as I kept my nose clean and said, 'yes sir, no sir, three bags full sir,' and this again was due to that good advice given to me by the scouser Mr Tarney.

On the way to Hatfield Borstal near Doncaster I palled up with a guy called Beldon from Leeds. Instead of sulking and being miserable and feeling sorry for yourself like most of the others, we were out for a laugh. When we arrived at Hatfield there were about eight of us. We all had to have a meeting with the governor, housemaster and a couple of screws. If Belly reads this he will remember this and have a laugh. We were all stood there, not allowed to talk. You could have heard a pin drop. In walked the governor. He must have come straight from the golf course, because he had his plus fours on, tucked into his yellow socks. He was quite portly and his glasses were on the end of his nose. Belly nudged me and whispered, 'Billy

Bunter.' Well, he was the spitting image of Billy Bunter and I started laughing.

One of the screws came up to me. 'You – one pace forward!' he screamed. 'Name?'

I said, 'Perkins.'

'Perkins what?'

I said, 'Harold Perkins.'

The screw was just about to land me one, after saying, 'Perkins "sir" when you speak to me!'

I found out soon enough the procedure was, 'Permission to speak, sir?' Then you always had to start by saying, 'With all due respect, sir.' When the governor said, 'What's the joke?' I said, 'Oh, it's just a private thing, sir.' So the meeting went on. Then five minutes later, Belly whispered 'Billy Bunter' again, at which I burst out laughing. I just could not control myself, and this was too much. 'One pace forward, Perkins!' I took one pace forward, but still chuckling, I couldn't stop.

The governor came up to me and said, 'This private joke of yours must be very funny. I think you should share it and we will all have a laugh. Now, what are you laughing at?'

'You sir,' I replied.

'What's funny about me?' said the governor, just as two screws came behind me. They were about to lift me off my feet for being insubordinate, when the governor said, 'Leave him,' and to me he said, 'So are you going to tell us what's funny about me?'

'You look like Billy Bunter, sir.'

The governor looked down at his plus fours and his yellow socks from over his glasses and said, 'You could be right, but I don't think it's funny.'

'Well, I did, sir.' I had overstepped the mark. You could not give your opinion unless you were given permission to speak and I had not been. I was lifted off my feet and marched to the 'block', a cell with no windows and a concrete block for a bed.

I thought, This is a fine start. I've been put in the block for speaking the truth. I should have kept my mouth shut – impossible. When you were insubordinate you were put in the block on bread and water for three days. I thought, When I get out in three days I am going to sew my mouth up. To my surprise, one hour later the key turned in the lock in the cell door. The screw said, 'The governor wants to see you.' I was marched at the double by two screws to the governor's office and stood to attention with a screw on either side. In came the governor, Billy Bunter, who dismissed the two screws, which was very unusual. He had changed from his plus fours and was wearing a suit.

'Permission to speak, sir?'

'Granted.'

'I would like to apologise, sir, but you asked me what I was laughing at and I told you the truth. I could have made up a story and lied to you, but I didn't, I told you the truth.'

The governor looked down at his desk top and for about thirty seconds it was complete silence, a long time in that situation. Eventually the governor chuckled and said, 'I think I can see your side of it now. In your eyes I probably did look like Billy Bunter.' He looked up at me and smiled. This was the first time I had seen anyone smile for at least six weeks.

Most of the governors and screws were sadistic bastards who got a thrill from giving you a good hiding when they knew you could not hit back, but this guy was a human being and a nice guy, and he liked me. So the two screws were beckoned and the governor told them not to put me in the block but to take me to my dorm. This was a dormitory in 'Wellington House', one of four. I was in number one, which contained twenty young men sleeping in one big bedroom. Belly was in dorm four, so I didn't know anyone to start with. The guy in the next bed came from the Black Country, Birmingham, and I couldn't understand what he was saying half the time. So I got talking to two lads who were southerners, Jim Bate and Nick Badman. Jim came from High Wycombe and was a very nice guy. Nick came from London, and I used to say to him, 'The people who speak the best, or the Queen's English, come from Yorkshire.' He always said, 'Rubbish. The Queen lives in London, so the Queen's English is spoken in London.' To which I used to say, 'Say bus.' He would say 'Bas.' I would say, 'Say butter.' He would say, 'Batter,' to which I would say, 'No more questions, your honour, I rest my case.'

I made a mate of Jim Bate. A saying in the north is 'our kid' and it's a friendly welcome, but Jim Bate said to me, 'Can you stop calling me kid? I feel as though you think I'm a goat.' When I stopped calling him 'our kid' we became very good friends. He was the only person I kept in touch with and went to see when I got back to the big wide world.

While I was at Hatfield I thought I had better knuckle down and act right in my head (a very hard thing to do). I was on my very best behaviour, another hard thing for me to do. I would volunteer for anything. I used to organise a ping-pong competition, and I initiated a collection of one penny a week off every inmate in Wellington House so we could buy a record that was in the top twenty hits. We used to hold a fixed vote on the record to be purchased. It was always the one I wanted, and one of the screws used to go into Thorne to buy the record.

This went on for a few weeks. I asked for permission to speak to the governor. When you asked to speak to the governor you had to state your case to the housemaster, and he decided. I told Mr Dean, the housemaster, that I wanted to borrow a bike and cycle into Thorne to buy the weekly record. He said, 'The governor is not that stupid to give you a bike and let you cycle out of here. We wouldn't see you again.' So my request to see the governor was rejected. A few days later I saw the governor and he stopped to talk to me. Although it was against the rules, I told him of my request and unexpectedly he liked the idea. He told me to put another request to Mr Dean and he would consider it. Well, to my surprise, he gave me a bike and permission to ride into Thorne to buy the weekly record.

This was something that had never been done before – give a convict a bike and a few shillings and send him on his way. Mr Dean was against it, and so were all the screws, but the governor's word was final. He trusted me, and on Saturday afternoon at two o'clock I was given a bike. The governor said, 'Don't let me down.' I was allowed one hour to ride into Thorne from Hatfield, buy the record and ride back. It took me only ten minutes into Thorne if I put my foot down, so I used to race to Thorne, buy the record, then go in the coffee bar next to the record shop with my borstal uniform on (they all knew where I was from), sit and sup a frothy coffee, then ride back to borstal. I arrived back five minutes early. Waiting for me at the gate were the governor, Mr Dean, and a couple of screws. Everyone except the governor seemed surprised that I had come back. Every Saturday afternoon it was regular for the borstal boy to be seen riding to Thorne and back. I was free for one hour every week and proud of what I had done – all thanks to the governor.

One guy I was matey with was a Geordie called Bill. He stoked the boilers up. I had the idea of pinching some spuds from the farmer's field next to the borstal and giving them to Bill to put on the shovel, then into the furnace, so we could have jacket potatoes for supper. I climbed over the wall, pulled some spuds up and took them to Bill in the boiler house. When I got to the boiler house Bill said someone had seen me and reported that I was doing a runner. I left the spuds with Bill and crept round the side of the dorm where the playing field was. In our dorm we had a table and four wooden chairs. One had been left at the edge of the playing field. I picked the chair up and walked back to my dormitory. When I got there I was greeted by a posse of screws and Mr Dean, the housemaster.

Mr Dean said, 'I have had a report that you were seen climbing over the wall to escape.'

'No, sir, I have just been out to get this chair that was left out this afternoon.' It was night time, about eight thirty and dark, and I said, 'They must have been mistaken. I never went over the wall, sir. All I did was pick the chair up. If I wanted to escape I would do it on a Saturday when they give me a bike.'

With this, Mr Dean said, 'Yes, you are right. Carry on.' That was a close shave – no more jacket potatoes for me.

I worked on the farm and eventually got the job of driving the tractor and trailer. It was considered the best job if you kept your nose clean. At harvest time we had to work over until eight o'clock at night. By the time we had finished, got back to the camp and had our supper (which was a mug of cocoa), it was nine o'clock. That was the time we had to be in bed, so we had no recreation whatsoever. We paid one penny a week for the privilege of using the games room and as we were working until eight o'clock we were not getting our value for money. Everyone who worked on the farm was complaining.

We put our case to the screws, but they said it was hard luck, we would have to put up with it. So I suggested to my mates that when they checked us on to the wagon after tea to go back to the farm we would stay put. After tea we all stood in a line, about twenty of us, on the parade ground. When they called your name out you were supposed to get on the wagon. Well, after half a dozen names were called out, 'Shonky Black', the screw who was calling the names, said, 'What's going on?' No one spoke. 'What's going on? Will someone tell me?'

So I raised my hand. 'Permission to speak, sir?'

'One step forward.'

So I took one step forward and said, 'It's about our recreation, sir. We think it's unfair that we have to pay one penny a week and get nothing for it.' Another screw who had been watching came over. They called him Bender – and you didn't muck about with Red Nose Bender.

When Shonky Black told Red Nose Bender what I had said I was marched at the double to the block. I was charged with mutiny and inciting a riot and sentenced to three days in the block on bread and water. I requested to see the governor and told him I was only speaking for the rest of the lads and that it was unfair to put me on bread and water for three days when I had been asked by Shonky Black to tell him what was going on. The governor agreed, and I only did one day on bread and water. I was beginning to like this guy, and I think he liked me.

Every morning at five thirty you were awakened by a screw, who would bang on the walls. The dorms were old army barracks, made of wood. He would shout, 'Hands off your cocks, and on your socks,' which meant you had to be out of bed and, come rain or snow, running round the parade ground for fifteen minutes. Then five minutes of press-ups, and woe betide anyone who tried to dodge the morning run, but it did wake you up.

I tried my best to keep out of trouble. But when you are in borstal if you're a goody-goody you get picked on. Eventually I got into a fight. Although I won I think the first prize was worse than the second prize. I got kicked in the goolies and was in so much pain I was admitted to the medical block and given an injection. My goolies became the size of a large grapefruit. When this news got round the camp everyone was coming to visit me and I thought I was the most popular guy in camp until I realised they were coming to take a look at this enormous goolie.

After a week in the medical block I got friendly with the MO. They called him Bland, and for a screw he wasn't a bad guy. One guy was admitted because he had scabies – a common skin disease in the early sixties 'inside'. This boy was a loudmouth, and I got the greatest pleasure from treating him. The MO said to me, 'Run a very hot bath for him and put half a bottle of Dettol in. Let him soak for fifteen minutes then scrub him with the big hard scrubbing brush.' Boy, did he scream. And that was the treatment for getting rid of scabies in the early sixties.

In Hatfield, as in any other borstal, the top dogs or 'daddies' were the hard men. The wimps were called 'susies'. The so-called rules or laws were made up by the daddies and woe betide anyone who didn't abide by their rules. There was a rule that said if you were inside for molesting a child, your life wasn't worth living, and I fully supported this. Now, the records of all the inmates were a close-guarded secret, and were always locked up and kept away from prying eyes. Just after I came out of the medical wing I had to have a light job, so I was a cleaner. This gave me access to the screws' office where all the records were kept. If you wanted to find something out about someone, I was the guy to ask.

Once you were in borstal you usually did all your time there unless you did a runner – then you were transferred to a closed borstal. But you were never transferred from a closed one to an open one. So we were all a bit suspicious when one Welsh lad got transferred from a closed borstal to Hatfield. Something like this would normally happen if you were in for molesting a child and the other inmates had found out. If they did, you would get a good hiding every day. Things would be added to your food and your cocoa at night would contain more urine than cocoa. A favourite trick was to get a razor blade, break it up into small pieces and insert it in his bar of soap. Everyone had their own soap, so it could not be seen. You can imagine the result when he was washing his face and neck.

Now the word went round that this Welsh guy was a child molester and he was going to get the treatment. I agreed with the treatment if he was guilty, but said, 'Suppose he has been sent here for something else?' We decided to put him on trial. He said they had made a mistake and sent him to a closed borstal when it should have been an open one. When they realised their mistake he was transferred to Hatfield after already doing six months in Rochester. We thought it had taken them a long time to find out they had made a mistake like that. So I said, 'There's one way to find out. I'll get his file when I clean the screws' office out.' I had to wait a few days for the right time. It had to be when there was no chance of a screw coming in and catching me, otherwise I would have been for the high jump. The time came a few days later, when Shonky

Black was on duty. He always used to say, 'I'm just popping to see the governor, I'll be back in thirty minutes.' What he meant was he was going over to the canteen for a cup of tea and a sly ciggie. So off Shonky went. I watched him go over the parade ground. Once he reached the other side I ran into the office and scanned the files for the Welshman's file. In the few days before I had access to the file, the Welshman had kept saying, 'It's true, you know, they made a mistake and sent me to the wrong borstal.' I opened his file and sure enough he was guilty. I put the file back.

When it came to recreation time after tea we held a court. I told the judge (one of the inmates) what I had seen in his report, and he was sentenced to the full monty. He got the works and the soap treatment as well. After reading that piece you probably think the treatment was a little bit strong, but that was the way it happened. If they dished that sort of sentence out today once they have been found guilty we would live in a far better world.

Although I have never been interested in football or cricket you had to play. I did enjoy playing 'murder ball'. This consisted of two teams, between ten and fifteen on each side. Each team would stand at the goals' ends and a medicine ball, a big one weighing about thirty pounds, would be placed in the centre of the pitch. When the ref blew his whistle, everyone ran for the ball. The object was to get the ball between your opponents' goalposts. There were no rules – anything went, punching, kicking, gouging... We used to play for an hour and after one hour at that game you knew you had played. I think the only reason there was a referee was to blow the whistle to start and end the game.

The only other sport I was involved in was canoeing. We were to paddle six canoes from Doncaster to Liverpool on the Leeds to Liverpool canal, but before we did this we had to train to be fit enough for the exercise. The training consisted of first running five miles, then ten to fifteen, and finally twenty-five miles. To start with there were about sixty lads entered, but only about eight finished the twenty-five mile run. I was never a good long-distance runner, but I did the twenty-five miles. After you had run twelve and a half miles they turned you round and you ran the same twelve and a half miles back.

Then there was circuit training. This took place in the gym. You were timed. It was a set exercise. You had to do twenty press-ups, twenty sit-ups, twenty pull-ups on the wall bars, along with another ten exercises. At the end of it you had to jump as high as you could and hit the wall with your right hand. You did this before you started. When you finished, if your mark on the wall wasn't higher than the first one you failed. After we had trained for over two months the project was cancelled. Never mind, it gave us something to do and kept us fit.

In borstal you were graded by the colour of your tie. It was a grey one for starters. A yellow one meant you were on your way home, and in between was a green one. This meant you had been a good lad and you were due one week's home leave. This normally came after you had served nine or ten months if you were a good boy. When I got to wear my green tie I thought, I am going to need some spending money for my week's home leave. Also with a green tie was Geordie Bill the boiler man, and we put our heads together to run some domino cards that were fixed. We won a few pounds for ourselves.

Once you got your yellow tie you knew you would be out in six to ten weeks. The way to get out early was to fix yourself up with a job. In those days, if they knew you had been in prison or borstal it was hard to get a job. They just would not employ you. So I wrote a letter to Matt Dixon at Mills Scaffolding asking if he had a job for me when I got out of borstal. To my surprise he sent a letter to the governor praising me to high heavens, saying what a good worker I had been and there was a job for me immediately. So with this glowing report I was on my way out. Good old Matt Dixon.

So on 23 December 1961 I was given the train fare to Bradford and taken to Doncaster railway station. I had done eleven months, three weeks and two days. Thanks once again to Mr Tarney — it would have been three years, but for your advice.

A Few Near Misses

So there I was back on civvy street. I had a serious talk with myself. I had been brought up on the wrong side of the street and as a small boy I had thought what I did was OK because everyone around me was doing the same. But I was old enough now to think for myself. I had just served nearly twelve months inside and it had done me good. I thought, I have been lucky enough to be given a job by Matt Dixon, and a well-paid one, so this is a new Harold Perkins. This wasn't the kid who would pick your pocket when you sneezed and your eyes were closed, or add a few pence to your shopping bill, or nick a few Woodbines out of your cig packet when you had just given him threepence for climbing down your cellar grate when you were locked out. Oh no, this Harold Perkins had turned over a new leaf. If anyone gave me too much change I would give them it back. This Harold Perkins would pay for petrol to put in the car, not milk it out of someone else's car for free.

If Matt Dixon and the governor of Hatfield and the probation officer had faith in me I wasn't going to let them down, and I was going to show them they were not wrong.

After I had been about twelve months at Mills Scaffolding, Matt Dixon got the manager's job at a firm in Leeds and he asked me if I would go and work for him. I took it as a compliment and I accepted. The new firm was called Norstel Scaffolding and they had all-aluminium scaffold, not the heavy steel and galvanised scaffold, so it wasn't as tiring by the end of the day.

One of the jobs I did for this company was Bradford Town Hall. In 1964 they were cleaning the stonework up, and it was a major operation. The clock tower alone was about 200 foot high to the peak. Working with me were Brian Muff, Barry Samuels and Albert Peters. We all used to have a laugh, especially with Brian. He used to catch the pigeons, and the next day when we were all eating our sandwiches Brian would be eating his pigeon pie.

When the scaffolding on the tower reached the height above the clock where the bells were housed, the best access up and down at break time was to go under the bells and down through a trap door. This was OK if the bells were not chiming. If they were, it was deafening. Our lunchtime was twelve thirty until one o'clock, so for a laugh I said, 'We will have lunch early to avoid the bells and the twelve chimes.' Just before the bells chimed you could hear the build-up for about thirty to forty seconds. So I used to try to time it so the lads were under the bells. I would go down the trap door, then lock it from underneath so they couldn't get down and they were trapped under the bells for the twelve deafening chimes. This worked only a couple of times before they got wise to it and started coming down five minutes before the chimes.

As it was a major operation and quite spectacular to see the Town Hall tower clad in scaffolding, we received a visit from a reporter from the Telegraph and Argus, who took a photo of us. So we were celebrities for a week or two.

There was a time when I thought my scaffolding days had come to an end. We were scaffolding one of the chimneys at the side of the lower. The pitch of the roof was very steep. In order not to crack any of the slates from the weight of the scaffolding we would put a batten (scaffold plank) under the saddle that went round the bottom of the chimney. We all knew that on roofs like this you had to be careful, as the slates had moss on them and were very slippery. I went down the roof holding on to the saddle scaffold to put the batten under the saddle. You had to lift the scaffold with one hand and place the batten with the other hand. As I was doing this I slipped and shot down the roof. From the chimney to the gutter was about thirty feet and from the gutter to the pavement below was about eighty feet. Now they always used to say that, if you were sliding down a roof, you should smash your heels into the slates. But the roof was very steep and I was going down at a fair old pace. At the bottom of the roof there was a gutter with a two-foot parapet. My feet landed sideways, jammed in the gutter, and the back of my boots trapped under the bottom set of slates, with the rest of my body hung over the parapet looking down on the pavement eighty feet below. After ten seconds I realised I wasn't going to make contact with the pavement and the lump in my throat was my rear end. It took about two minutes to prise my heels from under the slates – then it was back to work. I sent Brian Muff down the saddle to put the batten under the saddle. I wasn't going down that roof again and he had more bottle than me. That was one of my nine lives gone.

Another time I was working on a job at Greengates. It was wet and raining very heavily and I was trying to take a short cut down from the roof. Little did I know I was going down a lot faster than I had expected. I jumped from the flat dormer roof on to a blue slate roof, a distance of only about five feet. When a blue slate roof is dry you can walk about on it without too much trouble, but when the roof is wet and the rain gets into the moss on the slates it's like a skating rink. When my feet hit the slates they went up in the air. I was flat on my back and going down the roof at a fair old pace. Unlike the Town Hall roof that I slid down, this one did not have a two-foot parapet at the bottom. From where I had jumped on to the roof to the ground was about forty-five feet. Now, I was speeding down the roof and I knew I was going off and would probably kill myself. Why I did this I do not know, but I threw my arms up in the air and shouted, 'Geronimo!' That was the last thing I remember until I woke up in the hospital with a fractured skull and a damaged kidney. Seemingly I had hit the scaffolding on the way down and luckily had landed head-first in the garden, with my body on the concrete path and my head buried about eight inches into the soil, which was about nine or ten inch away from the concrete path. I dread to think of the result if I had been another few inches to the right.

When I woke up in hospital I could not see and could not talk as my face was swollen so much. My face was flat – my nose didn't stick out. My eyes were so swollen I could not open them and my lips were so big they still touched when I tried to open my mouth. So here I was in a lot of pain and I couldn't talk. I don't know what was the worst – the pain or not being able to talk. The next morning the nurse brought in a mirror and put it in front of my face. I could barely make out the image of a flat face with little slits for eyes.

The fall happened on a Sunday. By Friday I was fed up with lying in this hospital bed. I just wanted to get out. When the doctor came round in the morning I told him I wanted to go home but he said, 'No.' So I told him if he didn't discharge me I would discharge myself. He said, 'I'll do some checks on you at two o'clock this afternoon. If they show good I'll let you go home, but you go home and straight to bed, OK?' To which I said, 'Yes.' When two o'clock came the doctor came back, picked up my file, took my temperature, pulse, blood pressure, etc. He looked at me and said, 'You won't remember as you were unconscious when you came in, but I was the first person to attend you and saw how bad you were. Now I never gamble, but last Sunday, after seeing the state you were in, if someone had said to me, "I'll bet you a thousand pounds that guy will be out of here by Friday," I would have bet the thousand pounds. I have never seen anyone recover as quickly as you have, and I have been in this job for nearly thirty years. You must be made of something different from normal people.' Hearing that I was out of bed getting dressed, and the doctor said, 'Don't forget, straight to bed.'

Relief – I was going home. So into the car I got, with Sandra driving. At the time we lived on Old Road, Horton Bank top. As we approached Old Road, Sandra put the indicator on to turn left. I said, 'Straight on, we are going to the Royal Oak for a vodka. I've not had a vodka for nearly a week and it's two thirty now. Get your foot down.'

'But the doctor said—'

'Never mind what the doctor said.' So it was up to the Royal Oak in Queensbury for a few vodkas.

At that time, 1985, the landlord and landlady were Geoff and Celia.

Two weeks after I came out of hospital I still couldn't pick anything up without screaming pain going through my fingers. My local doctor sent me back to the hospital where I had my fingers X-rayed. They told me I had four broken fingers. I think in the rush to make sure I was treated for the fractured skull and the damaged kidney the hospital had overlooked my broken fingers, and it was too late to have them set. I did go for physiotherapy to get them moving again, and after a few months I could pick a vodka and tonic up without too much pain.

(1) Probably the first photo taken of Harold Perkins

(2) I can remember this one it, was taken at Jeromes on Tyrell Street and the photographer lent me the shirt

(3) School photo taken at Bradford Moor school

(4) Harold Perkins learning to smile

The original purpose of Linton Camp was not as a school, but as a holiday centre for deprived city children – but before it could operate as such, war was declared and the camp was taken over as an education centre. It opened in July 1940 and I joined the staff two months later.

The rest of the staff had all been reunited from Bradford schools and were all volunteers, and a more versatile and gifted lot of teachers I had never met. Besides teaching the basic subjects they could take country dancing (and later ballroom as well), needlework, handwork, music, games....

The school consisted of a series of long wooden huts constructed on concrete bases. There were two girls' dormitories, junior and senior, and two boys' likewise. The staff had their own rooms at the ends of each one. I had charge of the junior girls in dormitory 5.

AUSTERE: Linton Camp School as it looked in the 1950s

The huts were very austerely furnished with iron bunk beds and grey army blankets for the children and sheets sewn down the sides to form a bag. The staff bedrooms had a single iron bedstead, a chair and a large wooden chest for one's belongings which we promptly called a coffin.

Needless to say, we gradually refurbished our own rooms to make them more comfortable.

Opposite the dormitories were two wash places for girls and boys, with staff washing facilities at the back – so we had to troop across in all weathers to wash and shower the children and ourselves!

In the centre of the complex was a large hall, which also served as a dining room as it contained the kitchens.

At one end of this was the headmaster's room and at the other, the staff room – a very pleasant place with windows on three sides. Here we had our meals when not on duty and relaxed in the bit of spare time we had.

There was also a domestic science and craft block between the two sets of dormitories, and on the far side, the clinic, run by a Bradford school nurse – Nurse O'Conner, from Killarney, who became my greatest friend.

Alongside the clinic were two bungalows, one for the head and the other for the camp manager.

The last block of buildings was the classrooms. It was an extremely healthy life because we must have walked miles every day from one venue to another.

There were at least 200 children at any one time, and quite an odd assortment. When there didn't seem to be any danger of bombs in Bradford, the schoolroom became a dumping ground for all the misfits that the Education Department couldn't deal with.

We'd never heard of social workers, but that is what we turned into – and most of the children settled down.

One little boy, whose mother had died, had been caught stealing gloves and scarves in a Bradford store. A cry for help? He never stole anything at Linton.

Another was a German Jewish boy called Kurt Asch. His father had been a judge in Dusseldorf and had sent his children, a girl and a boy, to a wool merchant friend in Bradford, who in turn sent the girl to the Girls' Grammar School but sent Kurt to Linton Camp. Imagine the effect on that child who had been accustomed to a wealthy home. It took a lot of care and understanding to help him settle down.

Many years after the War ended, a very smart young man arrived at the headmaster's office and said in a strong American accent: "Do you remember me? I'm Kurt Asch". He owned a couple of restaurants in California!

During the first two years, we really had to do everything for these children – get them up, put them to bed, supervise washing and meals, teach them and keep them entertained and happy. We even darned their socks!

We had lessons in the morning and evenings, and kept the afternoons free for activities and games, walks, handwork, and darning. Every child at Linton learned to dance.

We often didn't come off duty until 9.30 or 10 o'clock after putting them to bed, reading them a story and waiting till they'd gone to sleep.

Then, in the summer, we went for bike rides as, with Double Summer Time, it was light until midnight.

We became a really happy family and the children meant a lot to us. I think I can honestly say that we were dedicated to them.

After the war, Bradford bought Linton Camp School so it continued to be a school for delicate and difficult children for several more years before it closed.

When I pass by the locked gate, I don't see ruined buildings. I hear the sounds of happy children playing, and school bells ringing.

● *This is an edited version of a feature which first appeared in the Craven Herald.*

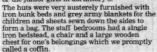

(5) Linton Camp

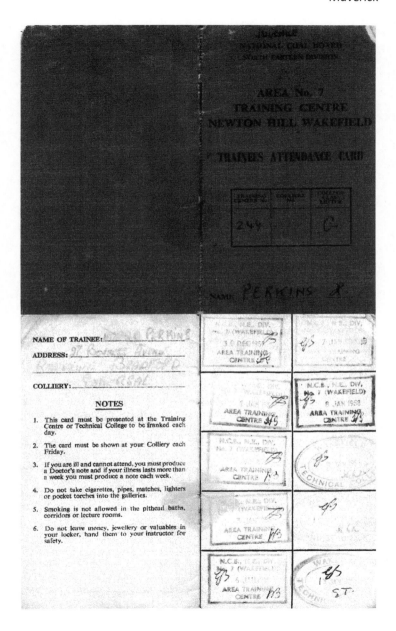

NAME OF TRAINEE: PERKINS

ADDRESS:

COLLIERY:

NOTES

1. This card must be presented at the Training Centre or Technical College to be franked each day.

2. The card must be shown at your Colliery each Friday.

3. If you are ill and cannot attend, you must produce a Doctor's note and if your illness lasts more than a week you must produce a note each week.

4. Do not take cigarettes, pipes, matches, lighters or pocket torches into the galleries.

5. Smoking is not allowed in the pithead baths, corridors or lecture rooms.

6. Do not leave money, jewellery or valuables in your locker, hand them to your instructor for safety.

N.C.B., N.E. DIV. (WAKEFIELD) ...FEB '58 AREA TRAINING CENTRE	26	N.C.B., N.E. DIV. (WAKEFIELD) 13 MAR '58 TRAINING CENTRE	WAKEFIELD TECHNICAL & ART COLLEGE
	N.C.B., N.E. DIV. No. 7 (WAKEFIELD) FEB '58 AREA TRAINING CENTRE	N.C.B., N.E. DIV. (WAKEFIELD) 14 MAR AREA TRAINING CENTRE	WAKEFIELD TECHNICAL & ART COLLEGE
WAKEFIELD	N.C.B., N.E. DIV. No. 7 (WAKEFIELD) FEB '58 AREA TRAINING CENTRE	N.C.B., N.E. DIV. (WAKEFIELD) 17 MAR '58 TRAINING CENTRE	WAKEFIELD TECHNICAL 24 MAR
TECHN	N.C.B., N.E. DIV. No. 7 (WAKEFIELD) 3 MAR 1958 AREA TRAINING CENTRE	N.C.B., N.E. DIV. No. 7 (WAKEFIELD) 1 8 MAR 1958 AREA TRAINING CENTRE	WAKEFIELD TECHNICAL & ART
	N.C.B., N.E. DIV. No. 7 (WAKEFIELD) 4 MAR 1958 AREA TRAINING CENTRE	N.C.B., N.E. DIV. No. 7 (WAKEFIELD) 1 9 MAR '58 AREA TRAINING CENTRE	WAKEFIELD TECHNICAL & ART
N.C.B., N.E. DIV. No. 7 (WAKEFIELD) 2 7 MAR '58 AREA TRAINING CENTRE			
N.C.B., N.E. DIV. No. 7 (WAKEFIELD) 2 8 MAR '58 AREA TRAINING CENTRE			
N.C.B., N.E. DIV. No. 7 (WAKEFIELD) 3 1 MAR 1958 AREA TRAINING CENTRE			
N.C.B., N.E. DIV. No. 7 (WAKEFIELD) 1 - APR 1958 AREA TRAINING CENTRE			
N.C.B., N.E. DIV. No. 7 (WAKEFIELD) 2 - APR 1958 AREA TRAINING CENTRE			

	CONDUCT RECORD	
	GOOD	BAD
	Appointed Group Captain 6/1/58 *[illegible]*	

(6) (5 photo's) Attendance card for' Newton Hill training centre, Wakefield. West Yorkshire

(7) (2 photo's) Harold Perkins at Belle Isle, Leeds

(8) Bradford Town Hall 1964

(9) Bradford Town Hall 1964. Harold Perkins with his team of scaffolders. Reproduced by kind permission of the Telegraph & Argus

(10) The Owls, Leeds Civic Centre

(11) Top left: Harold Perkins with Auntie Susan at Kew Gardens

(12) Harold Perkins 1963 with his pride and joy

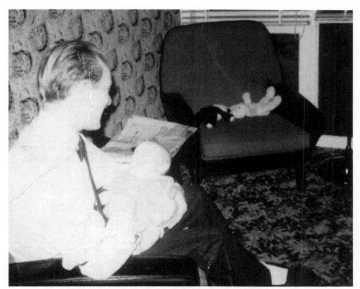

(13) Harold Perkins with baby Stacey

(14) Clockwise from top left, Stacey, Mary, Sammy, David

(15) Harold, Stacey and Mary 1967 Lands End

(16) David, Stacey and Harold Perkins with a hundred pound note

(17) Harold and Sandra at their wedding in Las Vegas

The Owls

Before the contract on the Town Hall was finished, Norstel said that they would be closing down their Leeds depot. So Matt Dixon decided to start his own scaffolding company with the guy who was the salesman for Norstel. He was called Adam All.

They set up and called it D&A Scaffolding Ltd, the D for Dixon and the A for All. It wasn't long before Adam All had had enough, leaving Matt Dixon to run the firm. He had asked me to work for him again, which I did. Although I had a business card with 'Mr H Perkins, Assistant Manager' on it, I was still a scaffolder working on the spanner. After a while Matt Dixon decided that all the work would be done on a price. This meant that if you got a price of sixty hours for a job and three of you did it in one day you shared it out, and you had earned twenty hours each. When I worked, I worked – I didn't leave something for tomorrow if it could be done today. The only person who would work with me was Peter Jack. This man was as strong as an ox and would work all hours. Usually on the scaffolding you worked in threes, two on the scaffold and one at the bottom, labouring. It was a lot harder if you worked a two-man gang instead of a three-man gang, but if you were willing to work that bit harder you would earn more money. My labourer could work horses into the ground. As well as working all the job out and supervising another three gangs I was on the spanner erecting scaffold with my faithful labourer, Peter.

About every three years the owls on the roof of Leeds Civic Centre would receive a coat of gold leaf paint. They were 150-foot high, and a scaffold was erected all round the tower to give the painters access. I gave this job to one gang on a price. At each side of the Civic Centre was one clock, at about eighty feet high, and one owl, at 150 feet. The procedure was to scaffold the clock, then while the painters were painting it you would scaffold the owl – then dismantle the clock, and then the same on the other side.

This gang on a price had scaffolded the first clock and said they couldn't make wages, and that, because I was dishing the jobs out, I was picking the best jobs for myself, which was untrue. So I gave them the job that Peter and I were down for working on the next day, and said Peter and I would do the owls. When we took over their job, it was twenty-two hours in debt. So Peter and I had to work a day for nothing to finish their job. When this was done the painters came on the job.

I had a word with the foreman painter and asked him if he would be happy with a platform suspended round the foot of the owls instead of scaffolding all the way round from the bottom. He agreed. So instead of the job taking a week, we would be able to do it in two days. To do this we would have to work from a 150-foot-high ledge that was only two feet wide. But knowing that we could earn a week's wage in two days spurred us on.

So instead of scaffolding all the way round we erected a scaffold tower inside to give us access to the two-foot ledge. We erected a tower to one side of the owl, then fastened two scaffold tubes that had to stick out four feet at the side of the owl's feet away from the tower. Having done this, I had to stand on a two-inch ledge that was approximately six feet above the two-foot ledge, with Peter holding my legs and pressing them against the building. I had to lean out and fasten two clips on to tubes that were stuck out past the owl's feet – not a very easy thing to do and a little bit dangerous. As I leaned out to fasten the clips, I said to Peter, 'Whatever you do, do not let go of me while I am leaning out.' With this I fastened the clips and climbed down on to the two-foot ledge which, after my standing on the two-inch ledge, looked as wide as a pavement. In order to hold me in to the tower, Peter had to put the side of his face against the stonework. You could see the small scratches on his cheek. I said to him, 'I could feel your hand shaking as you held me in.'

Peter said, 'Well, it is Monday, and I was on the beer all day Sunday.' We took a few chances, but we earned the money.

We once rigged some cradles up on two ten-storey blocks of flats in Leeds to give access for the painter to paint the outside of the windows. This involved pulling the scaffolding up eighty or ninety feet to the flat roof, erecting a scaffold on the roof and weighting it down so you could hang the cradles to the scaffold. The cradles were pulled up and down by means of ropes that went from top to bottom and through pulley wheels. Before the painter got into the cradles we always tested them to make sure they worked safely. One day we had moved a cradle from one side of the flats to the other, but we didn't have time to test it. So we said we would test it the next day. We always left the cradle at the top and pulled the rope up about twenty feet from the ground so no one could get into the cradles.

The next day Peter and I went up in the lift to the tenth floor and then out on to the roof. We climbed down into the cradle and started to lower it. The testing procedure was to traverse it backward and forwards, lower it down, then pull it back up to the top. We lowered it. When we got twenty feet down, the rope on my side as it came through the pulley revealed it had been burnt through. There were only a couple of threads holding it together. If these threads broke, we were goners. We were twenty feet from the top and eighty feet from the bottom. My first thought was to pull the cradle up to the top, but then I thought there would be more strain on the threads if we raised it, but less strain if we lowered it. If we lowered it, the further down we got the less far we had to fall if the rope broke. So we gingerly lowered the cradle down bit by bit so as not to put any strain on the couple of threads holding us up. We eventually got to the ground.

I have never been so glad to see the bottom of a ten-storey block of flats. We told the foreman painter, who contacted the police. They came and asked where the cradle had been when we left it the day before. We told him it was at the top. With this information they worked out on which floor the rope was burnt through. It turned out that one of the painters had been giving a married woman one on the sixth floor. Her husband had found out and thought this man would be getting into the cradle. We never found out what his sentence was and never met him, but he gave me and Peter a scare.

One day Peter and I had been working in the rain. We were soaked to the skin and had the job done for three o'clock. I said to Peter, 'Do you want to finish early, or shall we load the wagon for tomorrow's job?' As we were on a price for the jobs we did, the more time you spent working the more money you could earn. Peter said we would load the wagon. Wet through, we went to the yard at Clayton to load the wagon. Having loaded it in the pouring rain we set off home. At the time we both lived at Idle. I used to take the wagon home. It was about five o'clock by the time we set off.

We were behind a trolley bus at Lidget Green. The bus got through the traffic lights just as they changed to red. The bus stop was over the other side of the lights. As we sat in the cab of the wagon waiting for the lights to change, a man with callipers on his legs and two crutches started running across the road to catch the bus. He was running across the road where the traffic lights were at green, dodging through and round the traffic to catch the bus. The lights changed and we set off. The guy with the callipers, after dodging through the traffic, got to the bus stop as the bus set off. He was waving one of his crutches at the bus as it pulled away. Now I know you won't like this, but Peter and I started laughing and could not stop. Although we were soaked to the skin, freezing and tired, we still had the sense of humour to have a laugh.

Taking Snuff and a Laugh

One time I was working at Ossett, with Barry Samuels and Albert Peters, on a rainy Saturday morning. The scaffolding job was on a terrace house, front and back for the roof. Because it was raining heavily we called and had our breakfast on the way. We had just started putting the scaffold up when the lady of the house said, 'Would you like a cup of tea?' I said, 'No thank you, but we will have one when we have finished.' So when we were done she made us a cup of tea each.

We went into the kitchen and she said, 'I've put it in the front room.' I said, 'We are wet through – we can't go into your front room like this.' But she insisted, so we took our coats off and our boots and went into the front room, or 'parlour' as some people call it. Once in the parlour we sat down to our cups of tea and biscuits. Now, both Barry Samuels and Albert Peters took snuff.

Albert said to Barry, 'Have you any snuff? I've used all mine.'

'No,' said Barry, 'I'm going to get some on the way back.'

Albert got his empty tin out and started tapping the sides and bottom while holding the tin at an angle, seeing if there was any snuff stuck to the sides. This procedure gathered it up. There wasn't enough for them both to have a sniff.

Albert, who was stood up, walked over to the sideboard and said to Barry, 'This is a nice snuffbox.'

On the sideboard was a little silver box. Albert opened the lid and put two fingers in, sprinkled the snuff on to the back of his hand and sniffed.

Sammy said, 'What type is it?'

Albert said, 'Don't know. What do you think?'

Sammy put two fingers in the silver box and sprinkled it on his forehand and sniffed. 'Don't know,' said Sammy, 'but it tastes OK.' With this they had a few more sniffs.

We drank our tea, and the lady of the house came in for a chat. She sat down. We were all talking, when Albert said, 'This is a nice room.' The lady of the house said, 'Yes I often come in here and talk to my late husband. He died two years ago. I had him cremated and his ashes put in that silver box. I come in here and talk to him in the silver box and I'm sure he can hear me.' Albert looked at Sammy with his jaw wide open – they had just sniffed her late husband's ashes! I was dying to laugh, but dared not. Another embarrassing tale, but true.

Another job I did with Barry Samuels and Albert Peters was at Knottingley Tar Distillers. We had to erect a three-metre square tower round a steel chimney. It was about ninety feet high and they wanted to do some repairs to the top of the chimney. We worked until about twelve thirty, had something to eat for half an hour, then went back to work.

We put the ladders in as we went up and boarded the top lift out. The only thing left to be done was put the handrail and toe boards on, a fifteen-minute job, when Sammy said, 'I'll have to go for a pee.' I said, 'Can't you wait? We will be done in ten minutes.' Sammy said he couldn't wait, so I said to him, 'Pee down a tube. Nobody will see you up here.' So out it comes and into the tube, what a relief.

We worked away fixing the handrail. Then Albert shouted up, 'Maverick, how far are we from the sea?'

I said, 'About forty miles – why?'

Albert said, 'Well, it's started to rain and I can taste the salt in the rain.'

Well, all Sammy and I could do was laugh. We were still laughing when we got to the bottom of the scaffolding. Albert was still licking his lips and saying, 'There's definitely salt in the rain here in Knottingley.'

All the way back to Bradford in the car Albert kept saying, 'What are you two laughing at?' We couldn't speak for the fits of laughter, but eventually we told him. Albert said, 'You dirty bastards' – then started laughing. He had seen the funny side.

Occasionally the scaffolders would have a get-together or a booze-up as they called it. It was normally held in the Vic in Bolton Woods. One such time was Easter Monday or Tuesday. If you worked at Easter you were normally given half a day's work for a full day's pay, then you could go for a drink in the afternoon. So after doing half a day's work for a full day's pay we ended up in the Vic.

Now, I didn't know this, but they played a game called sing, sing or show your ring. Anyone who was in the tap room had to sing a song or drop their pants. Big Alan Goodenough stood at the door and no one got out. 'Maverick, you're first,' he said. Now, I thought, there is no way I am standing up in front of thirty men and singing, so I told them to get stuffed, or something like that. When big Alan walked over to me I stood up and tried to sing. I couldn't sing, so I said, 'I'll recite a poem.'

'You'll sing or show your ring,' said Big Alan Goodenough.

So I tried again. I managed to squeak a few lines of Roger Miller's 'King of the Road' to the disgust of everyone in the tap room. When Big Alan Goodenough said, 'That's enough of that. We can't listen to any more,' I was quite relieved. At least I didn't have to show my ring, and I now do a slightly better version of 'King of the Road'.

When I first worked with Alan Goodenough I thought his name was Goody, as everyone referred to him as that. When we played three-card brag at dinner time and there was just me and Alan left in, I would say, 'I'll see you,' and if his hand beat mine I used to say, 'That's good enough for me,' not knowing that was his name.

When he glared at me I didn't know why, until he said to me, 'If you say that one more time I'll throw you out of the window.' I thought, What have I said? The next time I said, 'That's good enough for me,' he reached across the table to grab me but I was up and off. When I asked one of the lads why he was so mad he said, 'He thinks you're taking the mickey out of his name.' When I found out that his name was Goodenough and Goody was the short version, I waited until he calmed down and apologised.

The Good, the Bad and the Ugly

I suppose when the word 'scaffolder' is mentioned most people will think of a big hairy-arsed builder going out on the booze every day and getting drunk and causing a fight. Well, most of the scaffolders I knew (and I still know some of them) were good, hard-working guys and family men. Here is a potted description of some of the guys I worked with.

Lewis Birkby and Martin Birkby were brothers, and good reliable workers who both liked to exaggerate, nice guys and excellent to work with. Martin's pockets were as deep as Lewis', whose favourite trick was to get a stone in his boot or stop to tie his bootlace so he wasn't first in the pub and would therefore have to buy a round.

One time when Lewis didn't get a stone in his boot was on a Saturday when about ten of us had been on the same job, finished at twelve thirty and headed for the Cricketers in Shipley. In those days there were no yellow lines, so you could park right outside the pub. I pulled up and was waiting for Lewis to tie his bootlace or get a stone out of his boot. But no, he was the first up to the bar and was ordering the round. Everyone was looking in amazement at Lewis getting this big round in. He even ordered two pints for two guys he knew in the other room. 'Thirty-two shillings,' said the barman.

At that, Lewis started fumbling for his money. 'Maverick, I must have dropped my wallet in your car. Gordon, get this round and I will give you it when I get my wallet.' So he went out to the car – no wallet. There never had been one. It was Lewis' way of getting a round in without paying. This time I thought, Good on you, Lewis, because the guy he had left to pay was Gordon Johnson, whose pockets were nearly as deep as Martin Birkby's, but not quite. We all thought Lewis had got one over on Gordon Johnson. But when Lewis came back into the pub saying he had lost his wallet with fifteen pounds in it, Gordon said, 'So you've no money at all Lewis?' To which Lewis said, 'I'm completely skint.' Gordon said, 'Well, the round came to thirty-two shillings. I'll give you the change I got from a fiver and on Thursday, when you get your wage, you give me a fiver.'

Nice one, Gordon. Lewis was stuck for words, and I'm sure the lads who were in there at the time will remember that little dodge.

Raymond Sutton, who now lives in Australia – what can I say about Raymond? I worked with Raymond on and off for a few years. He always wanted to be the boss, and thought he knew better than anyone else. He was a good worker and I got on OK with him. He wasn't the best scaffolder, but he was a grafter. You knew that if you were working with Raymond on a price you would be drawing good money.

When we worked for Palmer's Scaffolding I had their van, because Raymond had not passed his driving test. All the lads used to say, if he drives like he puts scaffold up, he'll never pass.

He had failed two or three times and had put in for his test again. He asked the supervisor at Palmer's if he could put learner plates on the van so I could take him out, to which the answer was yes. So I arranged to call and pick Raymond up after I had my tea. He lived at Union Road at Great Horton, and I lived at Idle, five or six miles away. I picked Raymond up, let him get in the driving seat and off we went.

He set off in first gear, but as we were going downhill he missed second and third gear and put it straight into fourth gear. So I told him to do it right – to which Raymond said, 'Who's driving, me or you? While I'm driving I'll drive my way.' I told him if he didn't do what I told him I wouldn't take him out. Raymond didn't like being told what to do and threw a huff. I wouldn't supervise him. He asked me if I would drive him down to Clifford Street, where you started your driving test from. So I drove him down in the van. The test guy came out. I confirmed that I had a licence and had brought him down. Raymond got in the driving seat and the examiner got in the passenger side and off they went.

The Labour Exchange was next to the test centre and our Tommy was there signing on. So while I was waiting for Raymond to return with a smile on his face I sat in our Tommy's van. I was telling him about Raymond and how many times he had been in for his test and failed, when I saw Palmer's van come round the corner with only Raymond in it on his own.

I jumped out of our Tommy's van and ran over to where Raymond was and said, 'Where's the examiner?'

Raymond said, 'He'll be walking down Manchester Road now.' He told me the story. It went like this: 'He took me up this narrow street and asked me to do a three-point turn. When I hit the pavement the second time I knew I had failed. I asked him if I had passed and he said, "I'll tell you when we get back to the test centre." Well I knew he would fail me, so I told him to f— off and walk back.'

I said to Raymond, 'Take me to this narrow street where you did the three-point turn, because if it's narrow he's out of order.' So Raymond took me up Manchester Road to Baxandall Street. I never got out to measure the width of the street, but I could have done a three-point turn in a seventeen-ton wagon and

Raymond was only in a five-hundredweight van. No more questions, your honour.

About twenty-five years later Sandra and I went over to see him. He took us to Sea World in Queensland – and when we came out of the car park he went the wrong way round the roundabout.

Bo Stevens. I think they broke the mould when they made Bo, one of the top scaffolders I have worked with. I got to know Bo when I first started at Mills Scaffold and always had the utmost respect for him. In the early sixties we went to work on scaffolding bridges when they were building the M6 motorway. We got lodgings in Crewe and the works bus picked you up at 6 a.m. to take you to Knutsford where we were about to start work. We were the last pick-up. When the bus arrived full of a load of navvies that we could smell before the bus arrived, we thought this wasn't the right way to start the first day at work, and we couldn't wait to get off the bus.

When we arrived, the foreman took us further into the site to tell us where he wanted the scaffolding on the concrete pillars. 'Where's the scaffolding?' we asked. 'I'll send it round on the dumper and you can have the dumper driver as a labourer.' Because we couldn't do anything until the scaffold arrived we sat down and smoked a few ciggies. One hour later the dumper arrived with what we thought was a load of scrap iron. 'I've brought you the scaffold for the bridge,' said the young lad, with an Irish accent. Bo and

I went over to the dumper, looked at all the bent tube, the fittings that had never seen a drop of oil and the battens that were split with no two the same length. We looked at one another and shook our heads, and Bo said to me, 'Are you thinking what I'm thinking?' 'Yes,' I said. With that we left the Irish dumper driver and his load of scrap iron and walked off the site.

It was about ten thirty and we were in the middle of nowhere. We walked for miles, then we saw a bus stop. We sat down at the bus stop and were having a smoke when a car pulled up. The driver popped his head out of the window and said, 'You've just missed the bus, and the next one's not due until tomorrow, they only run one a day.' He gave us a lift into the village, where we went into the pub, had a drink and a sandwich and phoned a taxi to take us back to our digs. So that was the start for the two travelling scaffolders.

Next day we boarded a train from Crewe and went to London. But at the time most of the building sites were on strike and there was no chance of getting past the pickets. So the next stop was Birmingham. We started work for John Laing's in the Bullring, just outside the railway station. We lodged in Erdington. We had only a ten-minute walk from the digs to the railway station in Erdington, then about thirty minutes' ride into Birmingham, and we were straight on the job. Better than Crewe and the M6.

The digs at Erdington were 'room only' – you had to feed yourself. There was a small kitchen in the room, but we used this only for making snacks. We used to eat out most of the time. One cafe that we used to frequent because they did a super breakfast was run by a husband and wife. The husband did the cooking, and his wife took the orders and the money and served the tea or coffee. Coming from Yorkshire, I had the habit of calling women 'love', and the girl in the cafe would say, 'It's two sugars in your tea?' and I would say, 'Yes, love.' It's a friendly saying in Yorkshire, but her husband in the kitchen thought it was too friendly, and let me know he didn't like it. When you have said, 'Yes love,' 'Thank you, love,' all the time it's very hard to stop saying it. After about two weeks of this, one morning we were in the cafe and I said, 'Thank you, love.'

The husband came out through the beaded curtain that led to the kitchen. He had a bread knife in his hand, and said, 'I am fed up with you calling my wife "love". If I hear it one more time I'll shove this knife right up your jacksy.' Even when I had spent about ten minutes trying to explain that I wasn't trying to get off with his wife he wouldn't have it. We had paid for our breakfasts so we stopped and ate them very quickly. Bo said to me, 'I think we should find another cafe.'

While we were in Birmingham I was still banned from driving. I had about twelve months left on the three-year ban, so I thought I would put in for my test and see if I could get another licence. I went to a driving school and said I needed some driving lessons as I wanted to apply for a full licence. I got a provisional license without any trouble (in those days there were no computers to check up on you). I told the driving instructor that I just needed a refresher course, as I had taken a few lessons when I was in Bradford.

On the day of my test the inspector took me round and did all the usual things. I thought I had done OK. On the way back to the test centre he said to me, 'Have you been driving abroad?' I thought I must have been near the white line in the middle of the road. Puzzled, I said, 'No.' Then the inspector said, 'You've driven very confidently for a learner. I thought you might have driven abroad.' Little did he know that I had a licence but had been banned.

We stayed and worked in Birmingham for about three or four months. Then we heard they were looking for scaffolders at Burghfield, a place just outside Reading in Berkshire, where they were supposed to make all the secret weapons. To get a job there you had to be vetted to make sure you weren't a spy. Bo and I passed with flying colours – how, I don't know – and we started work at Burghfield the following Monday.

Most of the building was underground with walls eight feet thick. Security was over the top. You could not walk over the grass – even if it took you out of your way you had to stick to the paths.

One time we were working on an underground building and I wanted to use the loo. Now the loo was about four minutes away if I went across the grass, but fifteen minutes if I went by walkways. I had a quick scan round to see where the security men with their dogs were. None to be seen. So I set off running across the grass. Two minutes later I was down on the grass with one Alsatian on one leg and another with my arm in its mouth. 'Don't move!' shouted one of the security guards. I thought, Don't worry, I'm staying put.

Two minutes later four security guards arrived and pulled the dogs off, but told me to stay on the ground. 'What do you think you are doing?' bellowed one of the guards.

'I'm just going to the toilet,' said I in a shaky voice.

'You know the rules here. You stick to the walkways, OK?' After taking my name and works number they let me go to the toilet, but not the short way. I had to go back, then all the way round. By the time I got to the toilet I'd forgotten what I was there for. We stuck the job at Burghfield for only about four or five weeks, because we were bored. All you did was hang around waiting until someone required some scaffolding, which sometimes could be a day and a half – and we were workers, not shirkers. So on the train and back up north we went. That was my time working with Bo Stevens – a great guy to work with, a top scaffolder and a good mate to go drinking with, until he had too much to drink and wanted to fight everyone. When it came to paying his round he was at the top, in Peter Jack's league.

Ronnie Greer, a Geordie and a good scaffolder. He came from the same village as Brian Muff, Bolton Woods, and was one of the old scaffolders, though not as old as Brian. When I worked at Mills Scaffold, Ronnie, who lived only ten minutes away, would walk down the hill to the depot at Mills. When he got there he always started coughing. At the time he wasn't even near thirty years old, but all he ever did was smoke and cough. Bo Stevens used to say, 'When he coughs he frightens the pigeons away.'

Brian Muff – a very good scaffolder, even better than me – was born and lived in Bolton Woods, and has done all his life. He couldn't keep up with Peter Jack when it came to drinking, but he wasn't far behind. The depth of his pockets was somewhere between Sammy's and Birkby's.

Once, Brian Muff and I were working on the Midland Hotel in Bradford. We had to cantilever and suspend a scaffold to give access to the stone gutter to renew the lead in the gutter. It was about eighty feet high. The cantilever wasn't a problem, but on the corner there were no windows to cantilever out of, which made it quite difficult. I said to Brian, 'What about if we put a tie round that big chimney, then send a couple of spurs down from the chimney to the corner of the scaffold to hold it up?' We had a discussion between ourselves as to whether the chimney was strong enough to hold the weight of a scaffolder going down the tube to erect the rest of the platform. We weren't sure, but we put the tie round the chimney and the spurs down to the scaffold, and hung a puncheon down on the corner, which was about five feet away from the building. A spur is a tube that goes from the chimney tie to hold the scaffolding secure, and the puncheon is a six-metre scaffold tube that is suspended from the scaffolding to give access. A scaffolder goes down the puncheon with only two inches to stand on to enable him and his mate to build the scaffold platform at the bottom. This type of scaffold is usually erected when access is needed only at the top of a building, usually eighty to 150-feet up, and it saves the expense of erecting all the scaffolding below.

The thing now was – who was going down the puncheon? If this tie round the chimney didn't hold, you were down eighty feet and dead for sure. 'You go down, Maverick,' said Brian. 'You are lighter than me.'

'Yes, Brian, but you've more bottle than me.' We discussed who was going down the puncheon and had not reached a decision by lunchtime, twelve thirty. Now I never drank at lunchtime unless the pub was the only place to go, and then it was only an odd one, but on this occasion there were five of us on the job and I got out-voted. We went for a liquid lunch in the Jacob's Well. After imbibing Dutch courage, when we got back to the job we were nearly fighting one another as to who would show the bravado and go down the eighty-foot high puncheon.

Unknown to us, some people drinking in the same pub, who worked on the third floor of the offices across the road, had been watching us erect the scaffold 'with hearts in our mouths' – their words. We told them the most dangerous bit was yet to come. This is why I think I let Brian go down the puncheon so he could show off to all the ladies who were watching him from over the road. He always liked that.

Peter Jack was the best of the nice guys, the finest labourer in Yorkshire, or maybe further afield. A proper boozer, he could drink everyone under the table, and his pockets were the shortest. His money used to jump out of his pocket and straight on to the bar.

Barry Samuels had to go into hospital for treatment for his skin complaint, psoriasis. He used to go in every six to eight months for his treatment, and I'm sure he enjoyed his stays. One particular time he came out with a very big smile on his face and said to me, 'My treatment after four days was to soak in a bath with some oil added to the bath water. After ten minutes I picked the soap up and started washing myself down. When I got to my naughty bits I washed it a bit longer than normal. At the time I was doing this, the nurse walked in and caught me at it. "Mr Samuels, what are you doing?" said the nurse. I replied, "It's mine, and I'll wash it as fast as I like." ' He told me the nurse helped him out.

Another mate of ours was Martin Birkby. Martin was renowned for having a tiddly dick, like a baby's arm holding an apple. We were erecting a scaffold inside the boiler at Elland Power Station and we could use the showers when the power station workers had done with them. On this occasion, myself, Sammy and Martin were waiting to go into the showers and the cleaners, who were a team of women, were waiting to go in and clean the shower room. We went in, and after about ten minutes the team of cleaners came in. Well, Sammy and I pulled the shower curtain on to hide our modesty, showered, put the towels round ourselves and scarpered from the shower to the changing room, only to look back and see Martin Birkby washing himself with the shower curtain open. The cleaner was mopping the same square metre in front of the shower that Martin was in over and over again, with Martin washing his baby's arm holding the apple and singing 'Zip-a-Dee-Doo-Dar'.

All these scaffolders had different characters. Martin was a nice guy and always fun at parties. He had to be, because he never got his hand in his pocket to buy a round. Albert Peters was a nice guy. He liked talking about the old times and his hobby was pulling women. He was an expert at it. Sammy was a good scaffolder and his interest in life was sending his lurcher to hunt rabbits while he was hunting women. His pockets were not quite as deep as Martin Birkby's, although they did go to the same tailor's. Sammy had a lurcher called Jack. At night and at weekends he would go out rabbiting with the dog. He used to tell me that when he caught a couple of rabbits he would bring them back and skin and gut them in the kitchen. He said Jack was a very hungry dog and would stand and watch Sammy while he skinned and gutted, knowing full well he was going to get the guts. One time Sammy had skinned and gutted two rabbits when the phone rang, so he went in the lounge to answer it. When he got back to the kitchen Jack had eaten both rabbits. He had probably thought, I caught them, I'll eat them.

Another tale about Jack. One Christmas, Sammy's wife, Helen, had baked some mince pies and left them on the kitchen table to cool off, but Jack got to them first and scoffed the lot. So Sammy said, 'I'll cure him.' When the newly baked mince pies came out of the oven red hot again, Sammy took one and threw it in the air for Jack. Jack leapt up, caught it in his mouth and swallowed it straight down. Sammy said, 'You should have seen the look on the dog's face when all four paws hit the floor.' He said Jack never ate anything that wasn't his after that – it cured him.

Roland Mathers was a supervisor at Mills Scaffold – a good scaffolder, and a hard worker and a nice guy. He wouldn't stand for any shirking or mucking about. When you worked for Roland, you worked, and if you ever had that privilege you had to move fast to keep up with him. And he always paid his round.

Jonathon Upton was Roland Mathers' grandson, a chip off the old block. I'm not sure how deep his pockets are as he's never bought us a drink.

Terry Ogden, my former business partner, was another good worker and a brilliant scaffolder. Although I worked with Terry for only a few years I have always had the utmost respect for him, even though he couldn't keep his eyes off the ladies. He always paid his round.

David Philp is in the league of scaffolders at the top, along with Bo Stevens, Peter Jack, Brian Muff, Terry Ogden, Barry Samuels and a few more. He's a scaffolding machine with a brain. Not only will he work all day long and longer if need be, he keeps everyone else working at the same pace. Nice guy, always pays his round, top man.

Martin Birkby was the life and the soul of the party. He always had a funny story or a tale to tell. He was a good worker and a splendid man. Martin and I worked together a few years and we always had a laugh and a joke. When Martin went on a site he always used to introduce himself to the site agent. One particular time, the site agent said to Martin, 'If you want to see the plans of where the scaffolding is going they are over there.' Martin went over and was studying the plans and saying, 'Oh yes, I can see exactly where the scaffolding has to go.' The agent came over and said, 'You've got the plans upside down.' Nice one Martin. Martin was a very good singer. He used to do a few Frank Sinatra songs, but he'll never be as good as me.

Andy Procter – a top man, good worker, honest and reliable with a sense of humour. When we used to go on holiday Andy would run the company while we were away and I always knew it would be in good hands. I think I had more faith in him than he did himself. Andy knew how to talk to the customers, how to keep them happy and the best way to do the job.

Peter Atkinson was a good scaffolder, an ex-supervisor who always did the job right, and a ladies man. Although he wasn't well liked among the scaffolders, probably because he didn't like shirkers, I always had a lot of respect for this guy. I didn't go to his funeral because I had to go to Sheffield to pick a part up for the van, which was urgent. I always remember thinking, If he's looking down he will be saying, 'Good on you, Maverick, work comes first.' Another nice guy who always paid his way.

Peter Wazerick was one of the first guys I worked with when I joined Mills scaffold. He came from Poland or the Ukraine and was a big, strong man. We were once working on a site together in Leeds and all day long all we did was carry scaffolding from one block of flats to the next one. It was boring so, to add a bit of excitement to the job, Peter said, 'For every scaffold board you can carry I will carry two more than you.' We set off. The carry was a good 100 yards, so it wasn't a short walk. I set off with two boards; Peter did four. I did four; Peter did six. And so on, until I tried to carry thirteen, hell of a weight. We got two forty-five-gallon drums and some breeze blocks and placed the blocks on top of the drums until it came to the height of your shoulder. This made the final lift a bit easier. Then I tried to carry thirteen boards to the next block of flats and managed about twenty steps before I had to drop the boards. But Peter carried his load all the way – a mammoth task.

Manchester and Ferrybridge

In the early sixties while still working for Mills Scaffold I got the urge to become a salesman, so when the vacancy of salesman for Mills Scaffold came up I thought I would apply for the position, I had a word with Matt Dixon who hired and fired but he said the position of salesman would have to go through the branch manager, so I applied for the position of salesman to the branch manager and a few days later I was in the yard loading scaffolding onto a wagon when Matt Dixon came out and said

"The branch manager wants to see you"

Now I thought this was to make an appointment for the interview, but no this was the interview and I was in my working clothes not looking smart as I would have if I had been allowed to go home and have a bath and put my best suit on.

When the branch manager told me he didn't think I was right material before I'd had the interview, I lost my rag a little bit and told him it was unfair of him not to let me get changed for the interview and that as I had spent several years in the scaffolding I could talk to the customer and advise them better than someone who had no scaffolding experience, but he said no and that was the end of being a salesman at Mills scaffold.

I think he was holding it against me because I had been in borstal and Matt Dixon had set me back on.

It was a while later when a friend of mine who had been a supervisor at Mills but had moved to a scaffolding company in Leeds told me they wanted a salesman to cover the northern area, so I put pen to paper and applied for the interview, and when I received a letter back to say they had granted me an interview I was over the moon, at the time I was scaffolding and earning one hundred and forty to one hundred and sixty pound a week which was very good money in those days and when I heard the salary for a salesman was one hundred pound a month and it was a month before you got paid and your commission was three month before you were paid I was beginning to have second thoughts, but the yearning to be a salesman won and I went for the first interview, when I found out that sixty three people had applied for the job I thought I have no chance.

At the first interview it was the branch manager and the field sales manager who interviewed me and my knowledge of scaffolding seemed to impress them, especially when I told them as I was a scaffold erector I could advise old and new customers how to erect the scaffold and even draw them a plan and work out how much scaffold they would need to hire.

Two weeks had gone by and not a word I thought the least they could have done was to send me a letter to say I had not got the job. Then I saw my mate Roland who told me about the job and he said I was still in the last six and would be going for another interview, a few days later I received a letter asking me to go for a second interview, I couldn't believe it.

At the second interview it was the branch manager, the field sales manager and the sales director who had flown up from London for the interview, for about three quarters of an hour they were all firing questions at me such as what would you do if you had an appointment booked with a customer and when you turned up in your smart suit and polished shoes and you had to tramp through the mud to get to his site office and when you got there he was in a bad mood and said he didn't have time to see me what would your reaction be. This came from the sales director and I replied that I would say

"Sorry I've called at a bad time I will ring you tomorrow to arrange another time"

To which the sales director said

"I don't think so, I think you would give him a piece of your mind for having you tramp through the mud in your polished shoes"

And when I told him he was wrong he just raised his eyebrows as though to say he was right. I thought there goes the job, then the sales director picked up the internal phone and ordered three coffees, I thought there are four of us why three coffees, so when the young lady secretary brought the three coffees in and didn't ask me if I wanted one I sad to the young lady I'll have milk and two sugars in mine, she looked at the sales director and he gave a slight nod with his head and I got my cup of coffee.

Now I thought the sales director didn't like me and I wasn't going to get the job so I told him I thought he had been very rude only ordering three coffees, I found out later he had done the same to the other five who applied for the job and they said nothing I was the only one to tell him he was rude and that was why I got the job.

I was doing very well but one hundred pound a month just wasn't enough, it was a week late going into my bank account and I got offered a job scaffolding at two hundred pounds a week although I was due some commission that wasn't due for another two months so I went back to scaffolding, you can imagine my surprise when nine weeks later I received a letter from head office to say my commission would be paid into my bank account and would be for six hundred and sixty pound and that was for three weeks as I didn't start until the eighth of the month, too late I was back scaffolding but I had proved the branch manager from Mills Scaffold wrong.

When I worked under Peter Atkinson (the foreman who gave me the nickname 'Maverick') he seemed a fair bloke. But a lot of the other scaffolders didn't like him, probably because he couldn't stand the scaffolders who had time off. This happened a lot if they had been on the booze and woken up next morning with a bad head. Being the site foreman he would dock your pay if you had a day off. I think he had a little bit of faith in me. When I did eventually have a day off for a genuine reason, the next week when I drew my wage I was expecting to be a day's wage short in the pay packet and I was quite surprised to find I had been paid. So I said to Peter Atkinson, 'I think they made a mistake – I've been paid too much.'

'No you haven't,' said Peter, and gave me a wink. Duncan, who was working on the same site, had taken a day off at the same time as me and was a day's pay short. This was when I knew Peter had some faith in me.

When work got a bit short, which happened at all scaffolding companies, they would put you working in the yard servicing the fittings or straightening tubes on less pay than working out on a job. One time when the work got short, Peter Atkinson said to me, 'Do you fancy going to work for Laing's in Manchester? You'd be on good wages and three pounds per week money for lodgings. We will be travelling it every day from Bradford and I will charge you one pound ten shillings a week for petrol, as we will be using my car. So you'll make one pound ten shillings profit.' I thought, this sounds good. So we used to travel to Manchester and back to Bradford every day of the week except Sundays. The team consisted of Peter Atkinson, Raymond Sutton and myself. We would leave Bradford at 6 a.m., stop for a quick cup of tea at a cafe in Oldham, and clock on at the site before 8 a.m. for Laing's on Miller Street, Manchester.

The job was the CIS building – at the time the highest building in Europe. Now Laing's had a bonus system worked on how many fittings you erected or dismantled. If you were erecting, at the end of the day the bonus man would come round and count how many fittings you had used. You would get seven minutes for erecting and three minutes for dismantling. When you were erecting you couldn't gain any fittings, but when you were dismantling, Peter Atkinson used to say to me, 'Instead of making one pile of fittings make about six different piles.' I couldn't figure why until the bonus man came round to count the fittings. When he had counted the first pile and went on to the next pile round the corner, Peter used to say to me, 'Take some of those fittings from the pile he has counted and put them on one of those piles that he can't see.' So this was the reason for making six piles instead of one. Doing this we got more bonus money. I was still learning. This was OK until the bonus man asked us to put them in one pile. When we did this I had to scout the site for spare fittings.

Eventually we got fed up with travelling all the way from Bradford to Manchester and back again. In those days before the M62 it would take one and a half hours on the old road.

We got a job nearer home. This was at Ferrybridge Power Station, which was only a half-hour drive from Bradford. They were building some new coolers. The firm we were working for was called Kier's. Their foreman scaffolder was a scouser called Wodel, and a right slave driver. We used to start at seven thirty and finish at six, and he used to say, 'If you want to work over until eight you can do.' If you were pulling your weight, after working ten and a half hours you were knackered, so we never volunteered to work over.

If we ever had to splice one tube into another we used swivels. For some reason at Kier's they used a fitting that we had never seen or heard of. They called it a side-by-side. But they didn't have any on site and were waiting for a delivery. We just couldn't wait for these side-by-sides to arrive to see what they looked like. Every day we used to say to the foreman, 'Have the side-by-sides arrived yet?' It was a standing joke. The main foreman was from Liverpool, and his right-hand man was a Londoner with a very strong London accent. When we asked him when the side-by-sides would be coming, he would say in his very broad cockney accent, 'If them fa—ing side by fa—ing sides don't get here soon I'll fa—ing phone fa—ing head office up.' We used to egg him on so he would spout off in his cockney voice.

My car at the time was a little Morris Minor. In my car travelling to work were Bo Stevens and Raymond Sutton. On the way home one night Raymond said, 'Stop.' I pulled up and Raymond got out of the car and ran back along the road. I hadn't noticed, but in the middle of the road lay a bag of carrots that had fallen from a wagon and had been run over a few times by passing cars and wagons. Some were only half squashed, and Raymond was picking the unsquashed halves up and putting them in his snap bag. He never missed a trick. The next night we were on our way home we again passed the carrots. By this time they were all squashed. We approached the roundabout and rat-eyed Raymond had spotted something else. It was a box on the grass on the roundabout. We went round three times but couldn't see what was in it, so I stopped the car, got out, went over to the box, opened it, and it was empty, Raymond shouted, 'What's in it?' I shouted back, 'It's full of side by fa—ing sides!' – which was another standing joke for the next few weeks.

When this fitting called a side-by-side did arrive we all inspected it, then used it. We worked it out that when you fastened one of these on to two scaffold tubes, the tubes were actually touching one another, hence the 'side-by-side'. You learn something every day. Working at Ferrybridge just wasn't the same as working on the town jobs – the jobs that you were on a price for, work hard, earn one-and-a-half-days' pay in a day and you were done for four thirty/five o'clock. So after about four months at Ferrybridge we headed for new territory. Just before we left, one of the scaffolders fell from the top of the cooler, which was 380 feet high. He hit the face of the cooler on the way down and he was probably dead before he hit the ground. His brother-in-law, who was working with him, had to identify him. The next day the brother-in-law came in to work and said the man had one of his knees sticking out of his chest. When something like that happens you think, 'That could have been me.' So for the next week or so we were all on our toes.

The Great Peter Jack

While at D&A Scaffolding, Peter and I were given a job to do in Leeds. It was only a small scaffold on a terrace house to renew the gutter. When we arrived on the job we didn't know whether it was to be put up at the front or at the back. We couldn't get hold of Matt Dixon, who had measured the job, and the lady in the house didn't know. All she knew was that the local joiner-cum-undertaker was doing the job and his place was just along the road. So off we went to the local joiner's place. When we got there his second-in-command said the boss would be back in twenty minutes – and did we want a cup of tea while we were waiting? We accepted the tea and stood watching him work. He was making a coffin. Peter said, 'He must be a big guy going in that one.' The joiner replied, 'Yes, but not as big as that one.' He pointed to one that had been finished and lined. It had been placed on two joiner's trestles and had the lid on. 'That one's another four inches longer than this one,' said the joiner. Peter was giving this larger coffin the once-over, and he said to the joiner, 'Can I get in it?' The joiner said, 'Yes, but you'll have to take your coat and your boots off.' Peter took his coat and boots off and climbed into the coffin. 'Mmm, quite cosy in here,' said Peter. I couldn't stand looking at him in the coffin so I went outside.

Eventually the boss turned up and told us where he wanted the scaffold, and we erected the scaffold for the gutter. For years after, every time I went on that road I always thought of Peter lying in that coffin.

One time Peter Jack and I had to erect a scaffolding on the gable of the chapel in Armley Prison in Leeds. This was completely different from erecting a scaffold anywhere else. You can imagine what would happen to the ladders if you left them lying about while you had your breakfast. Every time we had a break we had to collect all the loose scaffolding up, put it on the wagon, take the wagon through the prison gates and park it outside before we could have a break. Two prison officers stood there and watched us work, and as the week went by we got friendly with them and would have a cup of tea and a smoke with them in their staff canteen. One break time, when Peter had gone to the toilet, I had a word with the two prison officers and asked them if they would help me with a joke I was going to play on Peter. They asked what the joke would be, and I asked them if they could arrest him and lock him up for fifteen minutes. They agreed, but said they would get two other officers to do it, then it would be more realistic. So I told them his full name was Peter Jack and he lived at Idle. Peter came back from the toilet and we went back to work, I climbed up the scaffolding and Peter went outside the prison gates to fetch the wagon in.

He drove the wagon though the gates and pulled up to where we were working and got out of the wagon. Just as he got out, these two prison officers came over to Peter. One of them had a clipboard and a pen in his hand and said to Peter, 'Is your name Peter Jack?'

Peter said, 'Yes.'

'Do you live in Idle?' said the prison officer.

'Yes,' said Peter.

And with this they lifted Peter off his feet, said he was under arrest and took him to a cell. All I could hear Peter saying was, 'I think you have made a mistake – I've done nothing wrong.' Peter did see the funny side of it when twenty minutes later they released him and told him it was a joke.

One Saturday we were in the Waggoner's pub in Queensbury. As the night went on and the booze went down with ease, we got talking about how an egg can be delicate but also very strong. Peter Jack said to me, 'How can an egg be strong?' So I said to him that if you dropped an egg from 100 feet on to a grass lawn it wouldn't break, provided it didn't land on a stone or something sharp. 'Rubbish,' said Peter. After discussing the subject for another half hour Peter said, 'So if I throw an egg over my house roof and it lands on my lawn it won't break?' With this challenge on we set off for Peter's house – myself, Sandra, my wife, and Peter. By this time it was eleven thirty so when we got to Peter's house, first thing was to have a drink, then open the fridge and get the eggs out. After we had our drink we went outside armed with ten eggs. I lobbed an egg from the back of the house over the roof and on to the front lawn. I picked the egg up and it was all in one piece, not a scratch on it. Peter said, 'It's a trick, you've swapped it for a good one.' So I said to Peter, 'You stay on the front and I will throw one over and you will be able to see it come down.'

Peter stood at the front and after a few tries I managed to get one over the roof and on to the lawn, Peter just could not believe that it did not break. To finish the night off, Peter said, 'Just throw another over the roof again.' So with Peter at the front again I went round the back and lobbed an egg over the roof. Unbeknown to me Peter had put an egg in his pocket and, when the egg had landed, he took the egg he had in his pocket and squashed it all over his face and came running round saying, 'Look what you've done!' Well, we burst out laughing. By this time it was about 1 a.m. and most respectable people would be in bed, not chucking eggs over roofs. We must have woken the neighbours with all the noise we were making, because you could see all the lights being switched on and people peering out of their bedroom windows. That's when we stopped the egg throwing and went back inside for a drink.

We were always up to something. One time Peter was going on holiday and was flying out of Manchester Airport at 11.30 a.m. I said I would take him and his wife to the airport and would pick him up at eight thirty. Unbeknown to Peter I had arranged with a local farmer to hitch his trailer to his tractor, put a plastic table on it, with a parasol over the table, and set out a couple of plastic chairs which we borrowed from the pub. Then he was to go round to Peter's house and knock on his door and say I couldn't make it, but he would take them to the airport at Manchester. I had borrowed a mate's Rolls-Royce and a chauffeur's uniform complete with hat and was parked round the corner. The farmer pulled up outside Peter's house. Peter was looking out of the window and thought the tractor was going to the local school and had lost his way. Peter went outside and up to the farmer and said, 'Are you looking for the school?' The farmer said, 'No, I have come to take Mr and Mrs Jack to the airport.' Peter said, 'I'm not going on that – it will take hours.' The farmer said, 'I know a short cut over the fields.' Just then I pulled round the corner in the roller with my chauffeur's uniform on, let the window down and said, 'Taxi for Mr and Mrs Jack.'

Never a dull moment. I had borrowed the roller from a mate of mine called David Bull. He told me there was a leak on the brake fluid system and to keep an eye on it as it was going into the garage the next day. There was some brake fluid under the driver's seat to top up with. Well, we got to Manchester Airport, dropped Peter and his wife off in style, then parked the roller up in the multi-storey car park. We had a drink with them then Sandra and I went back to the roller. I had forgotten about topping up the brake fluid. We jumped in the roller and off we went. The way out of the multi-storey car park then was down the spiralling ramp at the end and out to the barrier, where you paid the fee. Then the attendant lifted the barrier and off you went. Well, halfway down the spiral ramp I put my foot on the brake and – nothing. The car was going faster and faster and the barrier was coming up fast. I was pumping the brake pedal and yanking the hand brake on. To my amazement we stopped with the radiator grille about two inches from the barrier. I had to put it in reverse to get back to the attendant to pay. He said, 'I thought you were going out without paying.' When I had paid the parking fee my first job was top up the brake fluid. Afterwards I thought, If Peter had been in as we were going down the spiral slope, he would have thought it was just another joke.

Another laugh we had with Peter was when we had all starred in a film by Albert Bateman called The Mind Boggles. It was about a guy who drank a lot and the more he drank the better-looking the landlady got. Peter was the main star. He was the one who ogled the landlady. She was made up to look ugly (when Peter was drinking his first pint) by making her teeth look black and putting scars on her face. As the night went on, and the more beer Peter had, the more make-up was removed from the landlady's face to make her better-looking. We all had our parts in the film, chosen by Albert. I was cast as the village spiv and Sandra as my moll. No one knew the full story, as Albert kept it secret until the premiere at the Bankfield Hotel near Bingley. It went down a treat, with Peter the star.

Webster's Brewery got to know about it and they asked to see it. Albert told Peter that Webster's wanted to see the film. I thought this would be a good time to pull Peter's leg.

It was at the time when Noel Edmonds would phone someone up and pretend he was someone else and 'have them on'. This used to be on the radio on a Sunday morning, and Peter would come in the Waggoner's on Sunday afternoon and say, 'Did you listen to Noel Edmonds? He wouldn't catch me out.' So I thought, Right. I had a word with a mate called Frank Walker. He was the one to do the Noel Edmonds bit. I wrote a script for Frank to say to Peter. It was at the time when Freddie Trueman was on the posters advertising Webster's beers. The script went something like this...

Frank rang Peter up and asked if he could speak to Mr Jack. Peter answered saying that he was Mr Jack. Frank said he was the advertising manager for Webster's brewery and he had heard that Peter had starred in a film showing him drinking Webster's beer, and he wondered if he would like to appear on a poster with Freddie Trueman. Peter jumped at the chance. Then Frank asked if he had been in the actors' union. Peter told him he was only in the scaffolders' union and that he hadn't paid his subs for two years, but he would bring them up to date.

Then Frank said that he was thinking of putting an advert on television with Freddie Trueman and Peter. Peter would not get any payment for the filming, but every time it appeared he would receive fifty pounds. At the moment it's on five times a night, seven nights a week. Regarding the poster, we will pay you five pound per poster, per month, and there are at this moment throughout Yorkshire about twelve hundred posters.' Peter did a quick calculation and worked out he would soon be a very rich man.

All the time Frank and Peter were talking I was recording the conversation on a small hand recorder. Peter told his daughter and two sons about the advert and posters with Freddie Trueman and they went round the village telling everyone. When Peter came in the Waggoner's on Sunday afternoon he was like a dog with two tails. He said, 'I'll get the drinks in,' and went on to tell us how the advertising manager from Webster's brewery had phoned him up and how he was going to appear on television and on posters with Freddie Trueman advertising Webster's beers – all because of the film The Mind Boggles. Well, we let him go on all afternoon and buy the beers to celebrate his newfound wealth. As the afternoon session was coming to an end, I got my tape recorder out, set it going and put it on the bar. 'Hello, could I speak to Mr Jack?' 'Mr Jack speaking...'

Once Peter heard that he looked at me and I said, 'So you would never be caught out by a Noel Edmonds trick?'

'Bastard!' came the reply. 'I've told the kids and they'll be telling everyone in Queensbury.' It took him a few months to live that one down.

On a bank holiday we always used to do a 'through' (drink all day and night). It was Easter Monday and we had an early start. At the time pubs shut at 3 p.m. and opened again at 5.30 p.m. so we had to find somewhere to drink for two and a half hours. We used to go to a club in Elland that we knew would be open. On this occasion we were driving back to Queensbury via Halifax and just approaching the roundabout at Bull Green, which was full of daffodils. Peter said, 'Look at those lovely daffodils. I wish I could take a bunch for the wife.' I stopped the car on the roundabout and waited for Peter to pick his bunch of daffodils. Then I saw two policemen tap Peter on the shoulder.

At this I sped off and parked round the corner near the police station. I thought it would be the last place they would look. I had a look to see how Peter was getting on. The coppers were making Peter plant the flowers back into the soil. When he had completed his task they gave him some verbal and let him go. I watched him walk away in the direction of North Bridge. I got in the car, stopped and picked him up,

'That was a near do,' said Peter. We had a laugh about it and went in the Royal Oak. We had just got in and ordered the drinks when Peter said, 'The police said to me, "What's your mate's name who was driving the car?" And I told them I didn't know. Then they said, "Where does he live?" So I said, "I think he lives at Queensbury." '

Thanks, Peter. I didn't live at Queensbury, but I did all my drinking there. So the next thing I did was go and hide my car out of sight. We laughed about that episode for years after.

Before we got to the Royal Oak on the way from Halifax, Peter said, 'Will you stop the car? I want to be sick.' Now this was something I had never seen before. I had known Peter a lot of years and had never seen him be sick through beer. He must have eaten a bad meat pie. I stopped the car and he was sick at the side of the road. He got back into the car, and I said, 'That's unusual for you to be sick.'

Peter said, 'Yes, I can count on both hands how many times I have been sick through booze.'

Sandra said, 'How many is that?'

Now, we were thinking eight, nine or ten at the most as that's the number of fingers and thumbs there are on both hands. 'Twelve times,' said Peter. When Sandra and I started laughing, Peter said, 'Honest, twelve times.' It was only when we made him count to twelve using both his hands that he saw the funny side.

Another time when we did a 'through' it was wintertime and thick with snow. We spent more time pushing the car out of snowdrifts than we did in the pub. We always did a tour round half a dozen pubs and if a new one opened we always tried it out. On this occasion we heard a new pub had opened in Thornton. When we eventually arrived we were all wet through. We ordered the drinks and sat in front of a big gas fire that was made to look like a real log fire. Peter's shoes and socks were wet, so he took them off and laid them in front of the 'log fire' to dry out. While Peter was looking at the layout of the pub, I took one of his shoes and placed it among the logs on the fire. When Peter turned round he looked at the fire and said, 'That's a nice fire, look at all those logs. It looks real, doesn't it? And look at that log, it looks like a shoe.' I said, 'It doesn't look like a shoe, it is a shoe, and it's yours.'

One time Peter had lent his van to the village tosser, and he had left it in a pub car park because it had broken down. Peter asked me if I'd run him over to where his van had broken down. When we got there we went in the pub and had a word with the landlord and thanked him for having the van parked on his car park. We said we were going to tow it to a garage to get it fixed. I said to Peter, 'Give me the keys, I'll try it.' So I put the key in the ignition. Nothing. I looked at the petrol gauge – it was on empty. Now I always used to carry a can of petrol in the boot for emergencies, so I poured the petrol into Peter's van, turned the key, and hey presto, the van started. Peter said the tank had been half full when he had lent it. The borrower had used all the petrol and was too tight to put some more petrol in so he had said it had broken down. What a tosser.

There was a time when I thought I'd my set my own window company up. The first customer was a guy in Wakefield who wanted his lounge window replacing in hardwood and double glazing. Peter, who was helping me out at the time, asked who was going to fit the window. I said, 'We are.' So we loaded the window on the van. It was quite a big window, eight foot long and four and half feet deep. Peter had never fitted a window before and neither had I, but Peter didn't know this. He said, 'How many windows have you fitted?'

I said, 'None. This will be the first.'

Peter started flapping and said, 'How can we fit this when we haven't fitted one before?'

'Easy,' I said. 'All you have to do is take your time and think about what you are doing.'

Before we started on the job I told Peter the first thing to do was to put dust sheets inside and outside the lounge window so that when we broke the glass it didn't go all over. Sods law, the guy had taken a day off work to watch us fit it. When I took the hammer and broke the big pane of glass, the customer said, 'I thought you would have put the glass cutter on it first?' I thought, This is all I need, the first window that I am attempting to fit and this guy knows more than me.

And he is standing over me. So I said, 'Yes, we used to cut the pane with a glass cutter, but a few months ago one of the fitters cut a big pane like this in half and it fell on him and nearly took his arm off. So now we use a hammer on them and break them into small pieces. It's far safer.' He agreed, and let us get on with the job.

So we fitted the window in. Next came the window board, the inside sill. I measured the old one and cut the new one just a fraction bigger and it fitted perfectly. Although it had taken us nearly all day to do it we made a good job of it and the customer said, 'It's nice to see a couple of workmen who take a pride in their work.' We cleaned up, had a cup of tea with the guy, and when we got in the van to go home, Peter said, 'I just don't believe that.'

Another tale I am going to tell about Peter Jack is when his daughter Ann got married. At the time Peter was working on the rigs and earning good money. When he came home for his two weeks off he would spend like a sailor, probably because he used to be one. When he got drunk, which was every night, he would throw his money about as though it was going out of fashion, and he wanted to buy drinks all the time. He would say, 'I'll get this round,' and throw a twenty-pound note on the bar.

I had a word with Brian, the landlord, and said to him, 'Just take the money, give it to me at the end of the night, and when he's sober tomorrow I'll give it back to him.' At the end of the night Brian gave me

£140. I said to Sandra, 'Put that in your bag until tomorrow.'

The next day, Saturday, was Ann and Bob's wedding day. We all met in the pub called the Fleece at the side of the register office. I got the round in, then Peter said to me, 'Can you lend me fifty pounds?' To which I replied, 'No, it serves you right for throwing your money about.' By this time Peter was in a flap – his daughter's wedding day and he had no money. 'I had two hundred pounds yesterday, I must have lost it.' I thought, I'll let him suffer a little bit longer. And then I said to Sandra, 'Give him his money.' Well, when Peter saw the £140 in twenty-pound notes he was delighted.

The night before we had all had too much to drink and all had bad heads. When we got to the pub at Thornton before going to the reception, Sandra went up to the bar and ordered our normal vodkas and asked for two glasses of water. Into the glasses of water we popped two Alka-Seltzers to try to relieve the headache. Unbeknown to us, Joe Brown was watching, and he thought we had put the Alka-Seltzers in the vodka, being the same colour as water. He came over and said, 'Is this a new drink? I've never seen that before – Alka-Seltzer and vodka.' When we explained that we had put the tablets in the water and not the vodka he saw the funny side of it.

The first time Peter Jack had an Indian curry was a bank holiday Saturday when we were on one of our 'throughs', drinking through the lunchtime session and the night time as well. The pubs had not opened for the night shift and the club was calling last orders, so I suggested that we should go for a curry as we could get a drink. Because Peter had never had a curry he could have a steak. So we went to the Indian Garden in Halifax. Sandra and I ordered a biryani with a medium curry sauce. Peter said, 'I'm going to try one of these curries – which is the strongest?' I said to Peter that as it was his first time he should start with a mild one like a korma or a bhuna, but no, Mr Jack was having the hottest curry they had. The waiter said he would bring him a phall, which was the strongest and hottest. We ordered some drinks and Peter was saying how he was looking forward to his first curry. Now, having a phall for your first curry, to me, was like going to Acapulco and diving off that cliff into the sea when you have never dived before and can't swim.

The waiter came with the meals, placed them on the table, and asked Peter if he required water, to which Peter said, 'No.' The waiter's eyebrows went up and he shrugged his shoulders, gestured with his hands and went away. We all got stuck into our meal. I said to Peter, 'OK?' Before Peter could answer me back he had to take a big sniff up the nose, 'Yes, I've only had three spoonfuls and it is making my nose run. I could do with some water.' I beckoned the waiter and asked for some water. There was a smile on the waiter's face and he said something in Indian that must have been, 'I told you so.' The water came, and the bottom of the water jug with about three pints of water in it didn't have time to touch the tablecloth. Peter had his glass ready. He filled it and downed the water in about three seconds, then another. A wipe of his eyes and nose – he asked me to wipe it as I was nearer to it than he was – and back to the curry. He would not give in.

I said to Peter, 'Leave it – at least you have tried it.'

'No chance. I'll finish it,' said Peter, and he kept at it with his eyes watering, his nose dripping. After three jugs of water (about nine pints, much to the waiter's delight) he finished his first curry.

The next day was Sunday, and we all used to meet in the Waggoner's on Sunday afternoon. Peter was usually the first of our team in by the time Sandra and myself arrived, but this Sunday I was surprised when we walked in and he wasn't propping the bar up. We ordered our drinks. Peter came through the door. He looked a little bit the worse for wear. When I asked him why he was late he said he had been on the toilet all morning. From his house, which was a ten-minute walk from the pub, it had taken him twenty minutes, as he had been walking 'three flags wide'.

So that's a few tales about Peter Jack, who's been a friend and workmate for nearly fifty years and is liked by everyone except his first two wives.

John and Hazel

I cannot talk about Queensbury without mentioning two very dear friends of ours, John and Hazel Morrell, with whom we have been friends for many, many years. We have had a few good laughs together.

One particular event I will never forget. It was a Friday night and we had been in the Old Hall at Denholme. We were on our way to the Royal Oak at Queensbury, John was in front of me in a big Datsun estate car and we were doing a good forty miles per hour as we went past The Raggalds pub. All of a sudden I saw John's car lift a little at the back. A wheel came out, but John was still driving along on three wheels. I blasted my horn and he slowed down. The wheel went past him and crashed into the wall on the other side of the road. Now we didn't want to start fixing the wheel back on as it was getting near closing time, so John put the wheel inside the car, locked the car, jumped in my car with Hazel, and off we went to the Royal Oak with John singing 'Three Wheels on my Wagon'.

As I say, John has been a friend for many years. When I fell forty-five feet off the roof and spent a week in hospital, John kept an eye on my business, and I have always been grateful for that. If I had to sum John up to someone who didn't know him, he's the type of guy who, if you had broken down at 4 a.m. on the motorway and it was a two-hour drive to get to you, and you rang him, he would say, 'I'll be there in two hours.'

Another of my favourite stories is the time we went to the Acapulco nightclub in Halifax with John and Hazel. Every time we went, John kept threatening to buy a massive bottle of champagne. It must have held two gallons, and John ordered it. There was no way we could get through all that bubbly, so John said to the waitress, 'Bring a few glasses and you and your colleagues can have a drink.' The waitress brought six glasses to the table and John filled them up. The waitress said, 'Cheers,' and took the drinks to her colleagues. Then she came back and said, 'You must be celebrating something special to buy such a large bottle of champagne.' Now I couldn't think of anything to say so I just said, 'Well I suppose it is special, really,' and made the following tale up. I said to the waitress that we had all been friends for years. I had caught John in bed with my wife, so to get my own back I took his wife to bed. We both divorced and married each other's wives and stayed friends. Everything had gone OK for a couple of years until John caught me with his wife, my first wife, so he started bothering with my wife, his first wife, and now we had got divorced and married our first wives again. That was what we were celebrating. Now, I didn't think for one moment she would believe this, but she did and said, 'Oh! How nice, what a lovely story.' She went all the way round the club telling everyone how we had been married, divorced, married, divorced and remarried. Every five minutes someone would come round to our table to look at who the strange foursome were. I just had to tell that one.

When John and Hazel were looking after the Waggoners pub while the landlord, Jack, was on holiday, one Sunday lunchtime John decided to put a cheese board on the bar. This contained about ten different flavours and types of cheese, with small name tags at the side of each. When Andrew and Jessica Fryer came in, John said to me, 'Just watch this.' He disappeared with the cheese board into the kitchen and came back with some more cheese on the board, plus some small pieces of turnip. He said to Andrew, 'That's a new cheese [pointing to the turnip]. It's very nice, try some.'

Andrew started eating the turnip and said, 'Very nice.' Over a period of ten to fifteen minutes he scoffed all the turnip, then said, 'Have you got some more of that new cheese?'

John said, 'You mean turnip.'

'No, that new cheese.'

Well, much as John guaranteed Andrew that it was turnip, he would not have it. It was the new cheese to him. We all had a good laugh at that one for many weeks.

Another time we had Andrew on was in the Old Hall at Denholme when Barmy Robert Balmford ran it. Every so often Robert would put a supper on. One time he said to me that the following week for Burns Night, and also his birthday, he would make a haggis curry. Now, I said, don't tell Andrew it's a curry as he will not eat it. Just say it's haggis stew. When they came in I said to Andrew, 'Robert's doing a haggis stew. Are you having some?'

'What's it taste like?' he said.

I said, 'Do you like oxtail soup?'

He said, 'Yes, I do.'

John agreed with me that this haggis stew that was really a curry tasted just like oxtail soup, so he had a big portion. When he finished it, I said, 'Like that?'

'Very nice, Harold, I could do another portion of that, very nice.' When I told him he had just eaten a curry meal, which he always said he did not like and would not eat even if he were starving, he said I was having him on. Even when John said it was a curry and the guy who made it said it was a curry, he still wouldn't believe it.

We once went to Malta for a short holiday with Andrew and Jessica and we ended up in a bar in Sliema called the Surf Side. In walked about fourteen young ladies and two men. Andrew was in his element when he found out that they were the Swedish women's football team. When they came in and sat down with us he couldn't wait to ask them what position they played and who the two men were (they were the trainer and manager). Did they all get into the shower together after the match? A couple of girls with smiles on their faces said, 'Yes.' He got a kick under the table from Jessica.

The Kentucky Fried Chicken story happened on a Saturday afternoon. Sandra and I had been for a few drinks and decided to have a take-out. I pulled up outside the shop and had to stride over two push bikes that had been left across the doorway, making it very difficult to get into and even harder to get out of. Going out you had nothing to lean against, whereas going in you did.

Stood inside at the counter were three young lads about fourteen or fifteen years old and an elderly couple in their seventies. As the couple were in front of the three lads, I thought, how are they going to climb over those bikes? I had just made it, and I was only thirty-five years old. I politely asked the lads if they would move their bikes as they were obstructing the doorway and people could not get in or out without great difficulty. To this I was told to sod off and mind my own business.

Now talking to me like that was their first mistake. I explained that the elderly couple would not be able to get out of the door, and if they didn't move them, I would. Just outside the shop was a really big bin to throw your empty food containers in. It was about six feet long and four feet wide, and I said, 'If those bikes are not moved in five seconds they are going into that bin.' For this I received another load of abuse.

I picked one of the bikes up and two of the lads tried to get it from me, but failed and it went into the bin. Before I could get hold of the other one to make a pair in the bin it had disappeared. I bought my Kentucky chicken and drove off.

The lads had taken my registration number and reported me to the police. On Monday afternoon a policeman came round to our house to interview me about the incident. I told him I had tripped up over the bikes as I tried to get out of the door and that must have been how the bikes had been damaged. On no account did I pick up a bike and ram it into the bin.

The policeman said he had witnesses to say they saw me ram it into the bin and one of them was the manager of the shop. I knew him, as I went in there on a regular basis, and could not believe he was on their side. I went up to see the manager and he said he had told the police he saw nothing. But the police took me to court and charged me. Now, I was suspicious of this manager, so I got to see his police statement and he swore my life away.

The next time I went for a Kentucky I had a quiet word with him, and he said he would not be going to court. When the time came for me to appear in court, I stood outside the courtroom with my solicitor, and he said to me, 'It's a pity that the shop manager will be turning up as now he's their only witness.' As it turned out, the shop manager didn't turn up, but the case didn't get thrown out either. The judge thought the witness had been got at, so they made another date for me to appear. This time they gave the manager a police escort from his home to the court and stood guard on him until he had given his evidence. Then he vanished. Needless to say I was found guilty, fined £100, and had to pay for the bikes' repairing and court costs. I would do the same again.

I did go to the Kentucky shop the next day but they had got a new manager. When I asked where the other one was, no one knew. Very strange.

The Good and the Bad

In the early 1970s, Peter Jack, Terry Ogden and myself worked for a scaffolding company in Bradford, which at the time employed about forty men as half of Bradford were having their dirty buildings cleaned. We worked on a price for the job so we used to start before anyone else, work harder and longer than anyone else and consequently earn more money.

The way they used to price a scaffolding in those days was in ten-foot by ten-foot squares, charging two pound and ten shillings a square: one pound per square for erecting, ten shillings a square for dismantling and one pound a square profit. You knew this only if you had worked on the management side, and I had. Most scaffolders didn't know the pricing system and could be fiddled out of some of their wages. It was harder to dupe me, and I showed Terry Ogden how to work the jobs out to make sure we were getting the right wages.

One week we were working on Salts Mill. It poured all day. Everyone except us called it a draw and went home. We worked all day and got soaked to the skin, and I mean absolutely wet through. Come pay day the following week we drew our wages and were a day's pay short. When we said we had worked all day in the rain carrying gear out we were called liars and didn't get our day's pay.

Another time at the same firm we had a job to take down in Chesterfield, a church tower, seventy feet round and eighty feet high. It was a day and a half's work. Peter Jack, whose car we were using, used to pick Terry Ogden up first as he lived in Wibsey, then pick me up in Idle. It was a Friday when we were given the job in Chesterfield. Peter, who was a keen Leeds United supporter, said he would like to get back on Saturday in time to go to Leeds to watch the match. So I asked Peter to pick Terry up at 3 a.m. and then pick me up. So with a very early start we went down to Chesterfield, took the scaffolding down so that we were due one and a half day's pay for each of us, and arrived back in Bradford in time for Peter to go and see his beloved Leeds United. I was in the Greengates Liberal Club with a drink in my hand and playing snooker at one thirty, and we had earned one and a half day's wages for a Saturday morning's work. Not bad, I thought, until the following Thursday wage day we pulled up outside the gaffer's house to collect our wages. Now, I didn't like this guy and he didn't like me, because I knew more about the job than he did. I used to ask Terry if he would go in and collect all the wages, which he did. Bear in mind I had shown Terry how to work the price of the jobs out – when Terry looked at the wages, he said, 'We are all forty pounds short.' To this, the gaffer said, 'Since you've been working with that Maverick you've got to know too much. You're all sacked – now sod off!'

Peter and I were sat in the car having a chinwag. Terry came to the car and got in the back seat and started laughing, and couldn't speak for laughing. Peter was looking at Terry, then me. Then we started laughing, but what were we laughing at? After about five or six minutes, I said to Terry, 'What are we all laughing at?'

In between chuckles, Terry said, 'We have been sacked.'

'What's funny about that?' I asked.

Terry said, 'I find it funny that you get sacked for being the most conscientious gang, the most reliable, the gang who does the most work and the only gang who worked all day in the rain and didn't get paid.'

At that firm, when it came to wage day, we always used to say, 'I wonder how much we will be robbed out of this week?'

He did me a good turn by sacking me. He got my goat up – an old Yorkshire saying, meaning he made me mad. Terry Ogden and I started our own scaffolding company, and a lot of his customers asked us to do their work. He accused us of robbing him of his customers, to which my reply was, 'They are only your customers while they are happy with you. When they find someone better they are not your customers.'

We were asked to give a price to scaffold a 150-foot mill chimney all the way round and right to the top for this firm to demolish the chimney. When we gave the guy the price, he said he could not afford it scaffolded all the way round, but could we give him a price for erecting an eight-foot-wide tower to the top of the chimney? I said this would be OK for inspection purposes but not for demolition. He agreed with this, so we erected an eight-foot-wide tower all the way up to the top of the chimney, with a working lift (a platform to stand on) five feet under the coping stones that went all around the top of the chimney. These coping stones weighed about half a ton each.

I knew what the demolition man had in mind. He was going to send a team of men up the scaffold tower to demolish the chimney by standing on top of it, knocking the bricks down inside the chimney, with a hole at the bottom so they would come outside. This would be OK, but first of all they'd have to loosen the six half-ton coping stones and send them down first – not an easy job. I said to the customer, 'Make sure those two copings above the tower platform go down the other side and not on to the tower,' as a half-ton coping dropping five feet would devastate the tower. With this I left him to get on with the job.

The next evening I was having my tea when the phone rang. It was the customer from Halifax asking if we could go look at the tower, as it had come away from the chimney. A helicopter had had to rescue the two men from the top of the chimney. I thought he was having me on until I was watching Scene at Six Thirty on Yorkshire Television. The newscaster said, 'We have just received news of a dramatic rescue from a 150 foot high chimney in Halifax.' I phoned Peter Jack up, as he had the wagon, then phoned Terry Ogden up. When we arrived at the chimney we looked up. The top of the scaffold had been pushed out by one of the coping stones.

Seemingly, when the demolition workers dislodged the coping, it had dropped on to the tower and pushed it away from the top of the chimney by about four feet. The men were stranded on top of the chimney and had to be rescued by helicopter.

So we climbed up the scaffolding to the top lift. I jumped from the scaffold on to the chimney and passed Terry some bars and sledgehammers that were hanging dangerously on the edge of the chimney, as we didn't want them dropping on us. Then we dismantled the two top lifts that were all bent and mangled with the weight of the coping stone, shoved the coping stone off and re-erected the scaffolding. Another job done.

Next day most of the papers carried the story about the two men being rescued from the chimney by helicopter when scaffolding collapsed. I had to hold my hand up to the customer – he took all the blame, and said, 'The scaffolding did not collapse, it was shoved away from the chimney when the coping stone fell on it.'

Terry Ogden, Peter Jack and I one Sunday had a scaffold to take down in Shipley. We all agreed to meet on the car park at the bottom of Bolton Road at five thirty in the morning. Terry and Peter parked their cars up and jumped into mine. I was just turning into Bolton Road when Terry saw a young mixed-race girl about twenty years old walking on her own. Terry wound the window down and asked her where she was going. She said she had been to an all-night party and was heading home to Shipley. As we were going to Shipley, Terry said, 'Jump in and we will drop you in the centre of Shipley.' So in she gets, telling us what a good time she had at the party. Terry and Peter were pulling her leg when Peter asked her if she had played any games at this party. She said, 'Oh yes, but they always want to play the same game every time.'

'What's that?' said Terry.

She said, 'It's called hide the sausage, and every time you know where they want to hide it.'

'Where's that?' asked Peter.

'In your knickers,' came the reply. We had never laughed so much so early on a Sunday morning.

There was a time when I owed the tax man six hundred and fifty pounds and I asked for time to pay which they refused and took me to county court. A company had gone bankrupt on me owing me a lot of money and this was the reason I could not pay, but the tax man didn't want to know and was very off hand with me. So I was summoned to attend the county court and while I was sat in this room waiting to go into the court room I got taking to the tax man and said

"Can we settle this without going into court"

I said I was willing to pay ten pound a week until the debt was paid off but he said

"Make it fifty or no deal"

I couldn't afford fifty pound a week so we ended up in court. I explained to the judge that I had offered ten pounds a week and could not really afford that as I was out of work (I wasn't) the tax man told the judge he wanted fifty pound a week and the judge said

"If he can barely afford ten pound he won't be able to afford fifty a week"

I was beginning to like this judge. The tax man wasn't very happy so the judge ordered me to pay ten pound a week and the cost of the court which was forty two pounds to be paid by me, now I said to the judge it wasn't my idea to come to court and if I was to pay the forty two pound I couldn't afford the ten pound a week, so with this the judge said to the tax man

" I suggest that you accept the ten pound a week and pay the court cost yourselves"

I could tell by the look on the judge's face that he was on my side and didn't like the tax man, because when he said that a little smile came to my face the judge looked at me and put his head to one side slightly as though he was saying to me

"Do you like that?"

The tax man agreed to pay the court cost and as we walked down the steps from the court I put my hand out to shake hands with the tax man and said

"No hard feelings"

To which the tax man told me to f... off and as I was going out of the main doors he said

"I'll get you, you bastard"

Needless to say I never saw hide or hair of him again. Thank you.

All went well for a while. A couple of firms went bust on us and a big cleaning company who owed us a lot of money refused to pay and delayed the payments. It took two years to get them to pay, and that was through a court. To this day they still owe us £11,000. By this time work was getting short and Terry and I had both had enough, so we parted company on good terms and went our separate ways. A nice guy to work with.

Years later I started in the scaffolding on my own. After trading for about two years I again got accused of stealing someone's customers, but this time I got burnt to the ground. My insurance premium was £11,000 a year and I thought I was covered for everything. I went to the insurance company and told them I had been burnt to the ground. One wagon, worth at the time £9,000, was completely destroyed and the other one was badly scorched. Scaffold worth £60,000 had been lost. They said, 'Were the wheels of the wagon in motion at the time of the fire?'

I said, 'No, the wagons were safely locked up in the garage.'

They said, 'Your scaffolding is only insured while you are transporting your scaffolding from your yard to the job you are doing, while it's being erected, while it's being dismantled and while it is transported back to your premises. But you are not covered while it is stored safely in your premises.' I thought, Why am I paying all that money a year for insurance that covers me only for when my scaffolding is being transported to the job? Who's going to rob a wagon while it's doing 50 mph down the M62 or while a gang of tough, hairy-arsed scaffolders are erecting the scaffold in the centre of Bradford or Huddersfield? But I am not covered while it is locked up safely inside a building? Most scaffolding companies stored their scaffolding outside in a yard, but at the time I stored mine inside as I thought it was safer. Another lesson had to be learnt. But I still had to have insurance cover, otherwise I couldn't trade. A few scaffolding companies didn't have the insurance cover and could do jobs cheaper, but I wouldn't go down that road. Many years later when we had grown a little bit bigger we had a quote from the same insurance company of £53,000 for the year. Can you imagine on a Monday morning thinking, before I do anything or think about making a profit, I have got to fork out more than £1,000 a week just for insurance?

When I started off in the scaffolding I had a pick-up truck that would carry only five hundredweight. I used to store the small amount of scaffolding I had in the outhouse. After a few months I stored it in the yard, but as we lived in a half-posh district I had to build a cover over it to conceal the view of the scaffolding. The pick-up that would only carry five hundredweight used to run on jobs carrying fifteen hundredweight. I used to say it went on the road begging, down on the back wheels because it was overloaded, but it did the job.

The first job I ever did was for a roofing firm in Bradford. They had won the contract to turn the slates on a big house in Pudsey, about eight miles from where I lived. Sammy and I loaded the pick-up with as much as we dared put on, and off we went to the job.

As we were working on the scaffold, the boss of the roofing firm came on the job to see how we were going on. When he saw the five hundredweight pick-up, he said, 'Where's your wagon?' Now, I couldn't afford a wagon as I had just started up, but he didn't know this, so I said, 'It's in the garage and they are waiting for a part to come, so hopefully it will be ready in a few days.' Jason, who owned the roofing company, said, 'You might as well borrow my wagon – I'm not using it at the moment.' Our faces lit up, because this meant we could do two trips with a seven-and-a-half tonner rather than twelve trips with the pick-up. Great. We used his wagon and the job was done quicker that expected.

Four weeks later when we went to dismantle the scaffolding, again we were in the little pick-up. Jason came along and said, 'Where's your wagon this time?'

'Back in the garage for a couple of days with the same complaint as last time,' said I, thinking, He's not going to believe it this time. 'You can borrow my wagon again, but only for a day.' Once again Jason had come to the rescue.

At the time I had a very small amount of scaffold, but most of the scaffolding on Jason's job I hired from Deborah's Scaffolding on a monthly basis. So with Jason's wagon it made it a lot easier to get back to Deborah's yard. That was my first job erected and dismantled, and I had negotiated a good price for a quick payment as I needed the money badly. True to his word, Jason paid me straight away.

My next job was down in Halifax again for a roofing firm, but this time I borrowed Ginger Jack's twenty-five hundredweight pick-up. Again Sammy and I did the job in a couple of half-days. When I first started I didn't have enough work to employ Sammy full-time, and the scaffolding company that he worked for only worked mornings. So after he had done his morning shift he would give me a hand in the afternoon.

When I wasn't putting the scaffold up I would put my suit and tie on and do my salesman's job calling on builders, roofers, joiners, demolition firms, anyone who used scaffolding. I called the firm 'HP Scaffolding'.

One time Sammy and I were doing a job at a pet food firm for a friend of mine called Ian Black. Ian and his wife Lynda ran an engineering company in Halifax. They wanted a scaffolding erected at the side and under the conveyor belt so they could work on it. At the time scaffolders never wore overalls or hard hats, but if you worked inside this firm you had to have the full monty. So I had to buy some second-hand overalls to make us look safe and official. The job was an awkward one and we had to jump or swing from one side of the conveyor to the other. In came one of Ian's foremen to see how we were doing. When he saw Sammy and me swinging and jumping about the scaffold like a couple of monkeys with our belt and spanners dangling from our waist he said, 'I thought it was the SAS, the way you were swinging about.' Little did he know he had just given me the new name of the company: 'SAS (Bradford) Limited', which stood for 'Scaffolding Access Services' and was a name that wasn't easy to forget. The next day I registered SAS (Bradford) Limited with Companies House in London. I had some business cards printed with a black background and gold letters and they looked impressive. When I was on my salesman's shift I would give them out with pride. It looked far better than 'HP Scaffolding'.

At the time all the scaffolding companies flew their own colours. They painted their tubes, fittings and boards so that if anyone stole their scaffolding they could identify it by the colour. Some chose blue and red, blue and white, black and red, green and yellow – you name it, everyone had a colour. The only colour that no one used, because it was too expensive to use on scaffolding, was a Hammerite gold. I had to be different, so I used to buy the Hammerite paint straight from the manufacturers in order to get it a bit cheaper. All the other scaffolding companies used to say I was mad to pay that sort of money to paint scaffold, but I had worked it out that, although a tin of Hammerite cost seven times as much as the paint they were using, once you put it on the scaffold tube it stayed on ten times longer. So in the long run it served me well, and I had a colour that no one else had.

It was a struggle for the first three to four years – not having any holidays, quite a few weeks with no pay, drawing the lads' wages on our Visa cards because some customers just took their time in paying, while others just would not pay and did a runner. When you first start in business, especially scaffolding, you always get the bad payers, the ones that no one else wants. They come to you until you find them out. It's OK if you can afford it, but when you're struggling it hits you hard. We managed to pull through, and eventually we sorted the good customers from the bad ones. We looked after them, gave them a very good service. I always made sure that if I promised the job would be finished and ready to work on by Thursday or Friday, it was always done for that time, even if it meant putting the spanners on myself.

One of the things I was very strict on was time-keeping. If you had promised your customer his job would be ready to work on, and it wasn't because some of your men had taken a couple of days off with a hangover, your customer would not be happy having to pay a dozen men's wages because your men had not finished the job. So when I set anyone on, I used to say, 'You are no good to me if you blob. If your mother dies you can have a day off; if your father dies you can have half a day off; and the first time you sleep in or blob because you've got a hangover, don't bother coming to work again, because you're sacked.' I only had to do this a couple of times before they realised I wasn't joking.

There was one guy who would get his wife to phone up and say, 'Paul's hurt his back and he can't even get out of bed, but if he's OK later on he will be in tomorrow.' Now I knew he had been on the booze and had a hangover, so I said to him, 'Look, Paul, you are no good to me if you have a bad back. I think we will have to look at your position here and I think you might have to go.' After this warning his back got better and he didn't have a day off work for about ten months. All the lads were calling me Dr Perkins because I had cured his bad back.

We paid top money for top men, and shirkers were not top men. Because we paid top money we were always getting phone calls from scaffolders wanting a job, but I only set them on if I knew how good they were or if they came recommended. It took a few years, but we ended up with some of the best scaffolders in the district. They were honest, reliable and hard workers, and for this they were rewarded with top wages. So, with assistance from all the lads, we grew into a reputable company that was known for doing a good job and being reliable.

When I first started the company I was told to advertise in the Yellow Pages, but it was £600 and I could not afford that. When I could afford it, we had that many good customers I didn't need to advertise. All our work came from customers who had recommended us to other companies. I was proud to say that, not only were we not in the Yellow Pages, we weren't even in the telephone directory. Very rarely did we put signs on jobs – all the work came by recommendation. Now, most scaffolding companies just do work within a 25-mile radius of their workplace, but we did work from Newcastle to London, Ashford in Kent, High Wycombe, Basildon, Norwich, Cambridge... Wherever a customer wanted us to go we went, and it worked out well.

I can remember one Friday I gave David Philp's gang a job for Saturday and Sunday. The job was on a building in Basildon and was definitely a two-day job with all the travelling. So, I thought, that's one team sorted out for the weekend. You can imagine my surprise when, at six o'clock on Sunday morning, I went to open the yard up and they were just pulling up with a fully loaded wagon. They had finished the job a day early. David said they had set off at 2 a.m., had their breakfast before they got to the job in Basildon, worked all through the day until ten o'clock at night to get the job down, had something to eat, and then set off back to Bradford, arriving at six o'clock Sunday morning. Then he asked what job I had for them that day. What a team! You don't get many scaffolders doing that. Needless to say they got double pay, plus a very generous bonus, and paid for working Sunday morning as well.

All the other local scaffolding companies used to say I paid my men too much, but they were worth every penny, and I enjoyed paying them good money. Nobody complained about their wages. One of my sayings was, 'If you're not happy with what I'm paying you, go work somewhere else.'

My customers were not just customers: quite a few became friends. We would go out for a meal and a few drinks and it was always a very enjoyable time. I think when it reaches the stage that your customers are also friends, you've made it in business.

The Family

I think this is going to be the hardest chapter that I have to write, because, to be honest and not pull any punches, it is going to shock some of the family. Here is the family tree starting with my mother and father, Kenneth and Rebecca Perkins, then their eldest first: Sheila Perkins, who married and became a Regan; my elder brother Tommy; and myself, Harold Perkins. Then along came the first to Alfred May, Carl, who took the name of Perkins until in later years he took his father's name of May. Then came Alan, whose father was the nightwatchman who kicked me down the cellar steps. His name should have been Allen, but he later took the name of May. Then came Susie, back again to Alfred May, then Andrea, Irene and last but not least, Georgie. All in all there were nine of us, from the same mother but a few different fathers.

Our Sheila died quite a few years ago. I didn't get on like a house on fire with Sheila, although I would call and see her when I was passing – she never came to see me. We never seemed like brother and sister. Sheila had climbed the ladder first and ended up talking posh, a thing I could never get my head round. When I used to ask her why she talked like that, she would say, 'I have to talk nice when I answer the phone at work as I am dealing with people who talk like this.' Sheila's husband, Paul, was a really nice guy, and so were all his family. I think the final straw came when I called to see her and she said, 'Our Martin is getting married. If you give me your address I will send you an invite to the do at night.' So I said, 'What about the actual wedding at the church, and the reception?' to which Sheila replied, 'Oh, the church and reception, yes, well, that is for relations and close friends.' Once she had said this and seen the look on my face, she realised what she had said: 'relations and close friends'. I was Martin's uncle. How more related can you get? Well, when the blushes had gone and she took in what she had said, she mumbled that the guest list had nothing to do with her. That's when I knew I wasn't her favourite brother.

The next on the list is our Tommy. I have always thought that if someone asked you to describe in one sentence what he is like and his attitude to life, it would have to be that he is against authority, against working, against anyone telling him what to do, and lazy. When he was in Feltham borstal I would write to him every month for three years. I didn't go and visit him as I couldn't afford the expense of travel and an overnight stop, so he did a full three years without a visit from anyone. When he went to borstal I would be about eleven or twelve, and when he came out three years later I hardly recognised him. He seemed to have gone from someone I knew to someone I didn't know. I think the time he spent in borstal changed him for the worse. He was a different person. It changed me, but for the better.

Here are a couple of tales about our Tommy. He wouldn't work. He signed on the dole for years. If they gave him a job interview, he would go and at the interview he would say, 'What time do you start?' The boss might say 7.30 or 8 a.m., to which he would say, 'Sorry, I can't start until 10 a.m.,' or, 'I can't work on a Monday, I have something to do.' The boss would write 'unsuitable' on the card that Tommy had to take back to the dole office to prove he had been for an interview, and he would be back drawing his dole money and not working. Because he signed on for so many years, most of the staff at the dole office were on first-name terms with him and when they wanted him to go to the counter they would simply call for 'Tommy'. One December he was actually invited to their Christmas party.

There was a time when he realised that if you were on the sick you got one pound and ten shillings more than being on the dole. If you could prove your injury had been done at work, you could get another pound on top of that. That was two pounds ten shillings more than the dole. This was too good a chance for our Tommy to miss, so he became self-employed. He went to the post office and bought one self-employed stamp, put it on his card, but didn't do any work. This would have been too much. Now he suffered from eczema, but only if he scrubbed the back of his hands with a Brillo pad. When he did this his hands would swell up and go all red. After doing this he went to the doctor and said, 'I was plastering under the sink for one of my customers and this is the result. I can't work with hands like this.' The doctor would give him a sick note and tell him to come back in four weeks to see if the cream had done any good. The day before he was due to see the doctor he would scrub his hands with the Brillo pad and the doctor would give him a note for another four weeks. After about four visits, the doctor would give him a sick note that lasted three months. This meant our Tommy didn't have to spend as much on Brillo pads as he did when he had to go every four weeks.

This went on for a few years. Then he received a letter from the Social Security to say that they would be willing to pay him a lump sum of £660 provided he did not claim on this again as an industrial injury. The reason I know the amount is I cashed the cheque for him. This was in the sixties, and £660 was a lot of money. So he pocketed the loot and signed back on the dole.

He is the only person I know who has never worked and has still been able to afford to buy a house of his own, although he did sell it and move into rented accommodation.

Another tale I remember about our Tommy was when he had borrowed a two-pound bag of sugar from his next-door neighbour. He said he would give it back when he had been to Morrison's supermarket. While he was doing the shopping in Morrison's he bumped into his next-door neighbour and gave him a two-pound bag of sugar. It wasn't until his neighbour got to the checkout that he realised he would have to pay for the bag of sugar he had loaned to our Tommy.

Although I used to pop in and see our Tommy, he hadn't been to see me for some years. I found out why. It was because six or seven years earlier he had called round with one of his grandsons. Now, we had a nice home and we had two leather chesterfield suites over which our Tommy's grandson climbed with his shoes on. I said, 'Will you tell him to stop that?' to which he said, 'He's only a kid.' When I insisted, he picked the kid up and went off in a huff. I was told some years later that, on that day, because I didn't want a kid climbing all over our chesterfield, he decided that he would never set foot in our house again. Someone in the family said to me, 'If you didn't go and see him, would he come and see you?' I thought, I'll try it out. So I stopped calling on him to see if he would call and see me. Ten years have passed and not a sign. You know the saying: you can choose your friends but not your relations.

Next on the list, our Carl. The least I say about him the better. He only wants to play cricket if it's his bat and ball and can take them home when he wants. He's very generous and friendly one minute, then tight and rude the next minute. I could never weigh him up.

Next our Alan. Although his father kicked me down the cellar steps, I could not hold that against him. When he was only seventeen, I was the assistant manager for D&A Scaffolding. Although you had to be eighteen years old to work in the building trade, I squeezed him in and put him on good wages. He was drawing between £40 and £50 pounds a week – not bad when his mates were drawing £10 or £11. He said to me if he took that sort of money home his dad would relieve him of it, so I used to make him another wage slip out that showed only £20. I told him to open a bank account and put his spare cash in it. He said, 'Can you open a bank account in your name for me? And then they won't find out how much I have in the bank.' (He was referring to his mum and dad.) I agreed, and opened a bank account in my name. Each week I would show him the bank book with the amount that was in.

This all went well until about seven weeks before Christmas, when he said he would like to draw some money out of the bank to buy Christmas presents. I said, 'Instead of putting the £25 or £30 you normally put in, use that to buy your presents. That way you won't be touching what you have in the bank.' He agreed.

Two or three weeks later I went on a job. A scaffolder who had been working with our Alan said, 'Well, Harold, I didn't think you were like that.'

'Like what?' I said.

'He told me that you have all his savings and won't let him have any of his own money.'

So with that I went to the bank, drew the money out (about £320, not bad for a young lad in the sixties) and gave him all his money back.

About five or six weeks later when he was at Garforth working with a guy called John on a school they were building, I called on the job and could not see our Alan anywhere. 'Where's Alan?' I asked John.

'He's gone home. He said it was too cold for him.'

I went round to his house at night time and said to him, 'The next time you walk off a job you're sacked.'

My mother was there and said, 'You can't sack him, he's your brother.'

I said, 'If he walks off a job again he's sacked,' and went out of the door.

The next day was a really cold day and the wind was blowing, so it made it feel colder than it was. I thought, I had better check on the job at Garforth. Sure enough, when I got to the job Alan was nowhere to be seen. 'Where's Alan?' I said.

'Gone home – it's too cold for him,' said John.

I went round to see him and told him he was sacked. My mother said, 'If you sack him, never darken my doorstep again.'

He still got the sack, and my mother didn't speak to me for six years. She would pass me in the village and ignore me completely, even when I tried to talk to her. She even ignored our Sheila, and when my big sister died she didn't go to her funeral.

On to our Susie. Married to Paul, she lives in Idle and has always been a worker. I think she takes after our mother, as she was a hard worker, not frightened to get stuck in and get the job done and calling a spade a spade. I have always got on well with her – probably until she reads the book.

Andrea next. What can I say about her? She's a hard worker also, always has two or three jobs going at the same time. I can't say a lot about her because we rarely see one another. It's usually at weddings and funerals, so short and sweet – not Andrea, the meetings.

The youngest female in the family is Irene. Again, I never see a lot of her. I think I've seen her half a dozen times in the past ten years. So not a lot I can say, only that when we do meet up we get on well together and she always seems cheerful enough.

Last and by no means least is our Georgie. He lives in Leicester with his wife, Mandy, both hard workers. He is a pigeon fancier; he has always liked birds. Although he lives in Leicester we get down to see him now and again and call and have a drink with them. I have always got on well with him and have a lot of respect for him, as he has always been a worker. If one job went down he would always have another job lined up in a few days. So that's the family tree of brothers and sisters.

Next on the list, direct family, starting with my first wife, Mary. I first met her before I did my stretch in borstal. She lived in a bedsit above where our Tommy lived, and I didn't like her. She always seemed a bit brassy to me. She was married, but not living with her husband, and she didn't appeal to me. After I had done my time and called round to see our Tommy, who had moved out of the bedsitter to a terrace house about half a mile away, who should be there? Yes, Mary, who had also moved out of the bedsitter and was living in a council flat on Thorpe Edge estate near Idle. Although she was older than me, and about eighteen months had gone by since I had last seen her, she seemed not quite as brassy. So I asked her if she would like to go to the pictures, then go for a drink. To my surprise she said yes, and I took her to the Ritz in Bradford, then to a bar. At the time I had a Rover 75 – the one with running boards on, used for standing on when you got in and out of the car. The doors opened the opposite way from now. It was the bee's knees, and I only paid £25 for it. I think Mary was impressed.

After we had been dating for a few months, I thought, This bird's got a two-bedroomed flat. Why don't I move myself in, as two can live as cheaply as one? So I did. We got on very well together. I was working as a scaffolder and Mary had a job at a firm called Flexion, so between us we had a good income and a good living. We eventually got married and started a family. She had a little girl from a previous relationship whom I always treated as one of my own. So here I was living with a married women with a four-year-old daughter. She was a worker, kept herself and the flat clean, and was a good cook. I thought, Why not tie the knot? But first Mary had to get a divorce from her first husband, John.

Although John was a big guy he had to bring his minder with him when he came to discuss the ins and outs of the divorce with Mary. When he said to me, 'I'll tell you a few tales about this women you are going to marry,' I told him to keep his mouth shut. At this his minder stood up and I said, 'You sit down and keep out of it, or you'll both go over that balcony.' The balcony was about forty feet from the ground. They sat down. Although they were both bigger than me I was only twenty-one years of age and a very strong and fit scaffolder. I think someone had told him I had a very short temper. So the ins and outs were sorted out and they left.

When the divorce finally came through, we got married at the register office in Manor Row, Bradford. I thought we were going to live happily ever after. It wasn't to be but that comes later.

I have three kids who have all done me proud and I love them all very dearly. Stacey is married to Tony, a scaffolder. Stacey runs a sandwich shop with her partner, Jackie, called Sandwich Experience on Cutler Heights lane in Bradford. Jackie is an old schoolmate. When I say 'old', I don't mean aged, although she is knocking on a bit. Stacey works very hard and has made a success of her business. Tony works for our old firm SAS (Scaffolding Access Services). They seem to get on together and they are always going on holiday, so they must be doing well. I think the reason that they have plenty of holidays is they have no kids.

Next down the line is our David. He works for himself, fitting windows, kitchens and conservatories, and he does a bit of plastering. I suppose you could call him a jack of all trades. He works very hard and can put his hand to most things. He's not married yet, but has a very nice girlfriend called Samantha, who has two little girls called Freya and Ella. David has two daughters, Kerrie and Laurie.

Last but by no means least, Samantha. She is the youngest of the three, married to Adam. They have two kids, Kelly and Thomas. The tale I tell about Kelly concerns the time when I wanted to speak to her mother and she answered the phone. She would have been about four years old. She said, 'Who's there?' I said, 'It's Granddad.' I heard our Sammy say, 'Who is it?' to Kelly and I heard her say, 'It's Granddad.' Now, she had two granddads, so our Sammy said, 'Which granddad?' To this she replied, 'It's the grumpy one.'

They run a sheet metal company, live in a fine house and have a place in Spain and a couple of smart cars.

I am proud of them all as they have all worked hard and done very well for themselves. They had a different start in life from their father's, so good luck to them all.

Things were going well. I had a nice wife, three lovely kids and was earning good money on the scaffolding. We used to go out on a Friday or a Saturday night when we could get a babysitter. Through the week I would pop down to the Liberal Club at Greengates, a men-only club with snooker tables. I used to enjoy having a game of snooker, then sitting round the bar and listening to old Bill Coates tell his tales of travel and recite a few of his ditties.

Mary started to go to bingo – not just a couple of times a week, but every night and every afternoon. It soon got to the stage where bingo came before anything else. I think the crunch came when I booked a meal at a restaurant to celebrate our anniversary. The table was reserved for nine o'clock. When I told Mary, she said, 'It will have to be after bingo.' Well, bingo didn't finish until nine thirty or nine forty-five. It was a twenty-minute drive from bingo to the restaurant, and the latest you could sit down at your table was nine fifteen. So I had to phone the restaurant and make some excuse about being ill. Bingo was winning every time. Every time I wanted to go for a night out it was after bingo. As a protest I went out on a Friday night to a working man's club at the other side of town. This is where I met my second-wife-to-be. In one way I should thank Mary and her bingo, because if it had not been for the bingo I would not have met Sandra.

I used to talk to Sandra, who would come to the club and sit down talking to her mates with her young son David, who would be about four years old. She was in a relationship at the time, but I didn't think she was happy. So I thought, I might be in with a chance here. When I asked her if she would like to go for a drink she said yes, so this was the result of the bingo sessions: I had gone off the rails. Now Sandra was fun to be with, and paid me plenty of attention, and we both enjoyed each other's company. Eventually she left her partner and I left Mary. This was one of the hardest things – no, I'll rephrase that – it was the hardest thing I have had to do in my life: leave my kids. I cried for weeks and weeks every time I thought about them. I did give it a second try with Mary because I missed my kids, but bingo won again, so Sandra and I became a permanent couple.

We lived together for nearly twenty-eight years, then went to Las Vegas for a holiday. As you know, you can get married at the drop of a hat in Las Vegas. But not for me. I was definitely not going to get married. That was firmly planted in my little brain. We went on the booze, got back to the hotel and, as we went up the escalator, I saw an advert that said, 'Do you know you can get married in this hotel?'

I said to Sandra, 'Did you see that?'

'See what?' came the reply.

'A notice that says you can get married in this hotel.'

'No, I didn't.'

So we went down the other escalator. On the way back up the escalator, I pointed out the advert.

Sandra said, 'What are you trying to say?'

I said, 'Well, what do you think?' I was drunk.

Off we went to see the preacher, who said that $140 would cover everything except the licence. So the $140 covered the ceremony, the limousine down to get the licence and the photos. I thought, That's not a bad do, so I paid and he gave me an envelope. I thought this was the receipt, but, when I opened it, inside was a slip that said, 'Contributions of $200 or more would be appreciated.' I thought, The cheeky bastard. Then, when we got in the limo, at the back of the driver's seat was a notice saying, 'Contributions of $100 or more would be appreciated.' I thought, Another one. Needless to say, they got sweet Fanny Adams.

When it was all over, I said, 'Where's the photographer?' The preacher said, 'She's been held up and will be here shortly.' Now there is one thing that winds me up, and that's waiting. I just cannot do it. After one hour of waiting for the photographer I said,

'I'm off.' Sandra said, 'You can't. We've got to have some photos taken.'

It was another half hour before she turned up. I wasn't a happy bunny. She said, 'Stand this way,' 'Stand that way,' and when she said to me, 'Smile,' I said, 'If you think after waiting one and a half hours for you to turn up I'm going to smile for you, no way.' The wedding photos are proof that I wouldn't smile for her.

All this happened on 9 April 2000 (I know because Sandra has just told me). When we got back to the UK everyone thought we had planned it, but we had not. That is how it happened. I did get accused of getting married in Las Vegas to avoid paying for a reception, so to prove them wrong a few weeks later we had the reception at the Raggalds at Queensbury, and everything went down very well.

Sandra's son, David, is a nice guy. We have always got on very well with one another. He's an electrical engineer who lives at Hipperholme, Halifax, with his wife, Kathi. They have two nice kids, Antonia and Ben, a couple of dogs, cats, rabbits, and Antonia has a horse.

I have had two mother-in-laws and both have been charming. Mary's mother, Emily, was a very nice person. She always had a smile on her face and a tale to tell and you could have a laugh and a joke with her. Clarice, Sandra's mother, who had lived at Great Horton, got married for the third time when she was seventy years old to a guy called Bramwell, whom she first met when she was sweet sixteen. His mother didn't approve of Clarice, and Bramwell went into the army, but they bumped into one another years later when their respective partners had passed away. So they got back together and got married. A nice ending.

Sandra didn't have any siblings, but Mary had two brothers and two sisters.

So that's a quick survey of the family. It just leaves my second wife Sandra. We get on well and seem to have the same taste in food, type of holidays, where to go and what to do. We even drink the same tipple: vodka and tonic. I've never been able to down a pint and keep it down. It must be because I have a very small mouth. We have been together for thirty-four years and still enjoy one another's company most times. All my kids love her to bits and there's no bitching or anything like that, which I think is brilliant. It's very rare that we fall out. I think it's because I agree with everything she says!

On one of our cruises we called at Lanzarote and had a walk round the local shops in the afternoon. We came across a Chinese restaurant that was closed, but we looked at the menu. We looked through the window and it seemed smart and clean, so Sandra said, 'Shall we have a meal here tonight instead of eating on the ship?' to which I agreed. So come evening time we disembarked and went looking for the Chinese. After thirty minutes we could not find it. I saw a policeman, approached him, and asked him in plain Yorkshire English if he knew where the Chinese restaurant was.

Now he could not speak English and I could not speak Spanish, so we were going nowhere quick. Then Sandra made slanty eyes with her fingers by pulling the corner of her eyes back and tried to speak in an English-Chinese voice. 'Ha!' said the policeman, 'Chinese restaurant, yes.' And because he could not tell us the way in English he took us right to the door. Brilliant. After that Sandra was going round telling everyone she was fluent in both Spanish and Chinese.

If anyone had to ask me what Sandra's claim to fame would be, I would say it was the time she refused (or was scared) to talk to Oliver Reed. Sandra and I had been out for a few drinks with Frank and Sylvia Walker, and Frank was a drinking pal of Oliver Reed. Frank had his own plane and used to fly over to Jersey or Guernsey to where Oliver Reed lived. This particular night we had been for a drink and gone back to Frank's. Sylvia put the television on, and who should be on it but Oliver Reed.

Sandra said, 'He's my favourite actor. I would love to meet him.'

Frank said, 'Would you like to talk to him?'

Sandra went giddy at the knees and said, 'Yes.'

Frank got on the phone and gave the secret password to speak to Oliver Reed, had a few words with him, and then said, 'My mate's wife is a big fan of yours and she would love to speak to you.' Oliver Reed agreed, and Frank held the phone out to Sandra, saying, 'It's Oliver – he wants a word with you.' This was when Sandra's knees started to shake and she said, 'Oh no, I can't.' So she had the chance to talk to her favourite star but never did.

We met Bob and Joan in Rhodes in 1983 and we have been friends with them ever since and they are like family to us, even though we live thousands of miles away we are still in contact with them and visit them when we can. They live in a lovely little village called Wooten Wawen near to Henley in Arden.

A Few More Friends

In the late sixties, work on the scaffolding was very sparse, and I was laid off. I phoned a few scaffolding companies but they were all in the same boat. I was just about to start a job on the Monday morning at a foundry, stoking the furnace up. You had to start at 6 a.m. and finish at 6 p.m., five shifts a week. The wage was £18 a week, but it was better than being on the dole.

I was in the Sun club on the Sunday night talking to Samuel Lements, who was a double glazing salesman. In the sixties very few people had heard about double glazing. Samuel said to me, 'Why don't you give it a go? It will be better than working in a foundry for £18 a week.' After a few more drinks I thought I would give it a go. Samuel said I had to be at the office at 10 a.m. I thought, That's better than 6 a.m., so with my best suit, shirt and tie on I turned up at the office at the bottom of Sunbridge Road at nine fifty-five for the interview. A guy called Edward interviewed me. He said he thought I could do the job. Did I want to start that day and come back at four o'clock, the time they started? I thought this was a funny time to start work. Edward explained that we would be knocking on people's doors, and through the day they would be at work. At evening time they would be in. When I thought about it, it made sense. So I started the same day at four o'clock.

I was working with a guy called Frank Southworth, who showed me the ropes. Although you had to tramp round knocking on doors in wind, hail or rain, I quite enjoyed it, and soon made my way up from a canvasser to a salesman. Most nights you were done by nine o'clock, so the hours were very good. The first week I worked I drew only £12, but the next week I drew £22 and six weeks later, because I was on a commission, I drew £46. Yes, this was the job for me.

I worked for this firm for about six months. It was the time when our David had been run over and had a broken thigh. He had just come out of Woodlands Hospital at Rawdon and I had to take him to Bradford Royal Infirmary to have his plaster removed. I had to lay him across the back seat because he could not bend his leg. On the way to the infirmary I called to pick Frank Southworth up to drop him at work. I introduced our David, who was only three and half years old at the time. I said, 'This is Frank. I work with him.' When I dropped Frank off at the office he said, 'Bye, David, see you later,' to which our David said, 'Goodbye,

Mr Stein.' He thought because they called him Frank he was Mr Frankenstein. Frank saw the funny side of it. It wasn't until a few hours later I thought our David wasn't far out. He did look a bit like Frankenstein's monster.

After about six months with this firm, I was told by a guy called Matt Price that he knew a man who had just started his own double glazing company. He paid good money and didn't rob you like all the rest. It was a firm called SGS, run by a guy called Barrie Stamper. Off I went and started at this new firm. The first few weeks I didn't do brilliantly. As you were on commission, the more you sold the bigger wage you would get. After about five or six weeks I had got into their way of selling and was earning quite good money. I was soon running a nice Jaguar car and working only a few hours a night. I got on quite well with the guy who owned the company. We used to go for a drink at the weekend and have a laugh and a joke. He was another nice and generous guy.

A few years later two guys came to work at SGS called Frank Walker – the same guy mentioned earlier – and David Bull. They were very good salesmen and also knew how to enjoy themselves. When you went out for a drink with Frank and David it wasn't a couple of hours, it was a couple of days.

One time we were all working in Pudsey and had agreed to meet up when we finished in a new wine bar called Fanny by Gaslight. This wine bar, as you can guess by the name, was decorated and themed in line with the Victorian era. At the top of the stairs they had a mannequin dressed up in Victorian clothes. We had been in the bar a few times so the owner knew us and was aware we were good spenders. We had been in early doors and had a few when Frank said, 'Can I borrow the dummy?' The owner said no, but Frank and David said they would leave £100 as security. She succumbed, and they carried it out and put it in the car. We took it into work and sat it in the boardroom. Then I had the idea of buying a pair of crotchless knickers which we put on the dummy. We pulled her skirt up, bent her over the boardroom table and put a whip in her hand. Frank, David and myself were having a good laugh about this when Vola, who worked in the office, came in and said, 'Barrie is on his way over.' Barrie, the main director, had his office in one of the other buildings and very rarely came over to ours. Frank said, 'If Barrie sees that in the boardroom we'll be in for it. Harold, you keep Barrie talking on the steps and, Vola, you take the dummy down the fire escape and put it in the boot of David's car.' I watched Barrie walk across the yard, gave him time to open the door, then started walking down the stairs to meet Barrie halfway.

'Hi! Barrie, how you doing?' I said. 'Haven't seen you for a while. We will have to go out for a drink over at the club.' We used to go and play cards every Saturday night at the Liberal Club at Greengates, but since I had left my first wife, Mary, we hadn't been. I was making small talk to give Vola time to get the mannequin down the fire escape and into David's car boot. I was halfway down the stairs and I could see through the window above the door that Vola was having trouble getting the dummy in the boot of David's car. He had got her in except for one leg that was sticking out and showing her crotchless knickers. I knew if Barrie went into Frank's office he would be able to see Vola through the window at the back of Frank's desk. I could tell by the way Barrie had walked briskly across the yard and from the look on his face he was not in a good mood. If he saw the dummy he would be fuming.

Eventually Vola got the mannequin in the boot and I stopped talking to Barrie. He went up the stairs to have a meeting with Frank and David in the boardroom. But this was not the end of the dummy saga.

One Saturday afternoon Frank and David decided to take the mannequin into Bradford for a drink. They took it to Alan Jubb's pub, down at the bottom of Ivegate, called the Old Crown. They took it into the pub and leaned it on the bar. They even bought her a drink. After a full session of about four hours they got hold of her, Frank at one side and David at the other, and walked her out of the pub and up Ivegate, stopping every thirty paces to give her a smack on the backside by lifting her skirt up and hitting her with the whip. An old lady had seen them and thought they were hitting a real woman. She phoned the police, who were waiting for Frank and David at the top of Ivegate. You can imagine the look on the officers' faces when they saw it was a mannequin and not a human being. They saw the funny side of it.

The final episode of the dummy saga was about three months after she was returned to the Fanny by Gaslight bar. Sandra and I were in the Karachi curry house queuing up for a takeaway because the restaurant was too full for us to eat there. There were about ten people in front of us and a dozen behind us, when a woman said to me, 'Hi, I bet you don't recognise me.' I looked at her and I had never seen her before in my life. I said, 'Sorry, you must have the wrong guy, you're mistaken.' She said, 'I don't think so.'

I had had a few drinks, but this lady had had a few more than me and was speaking quite loudly. She continued and said, 'Yes, it's you, I remember you. I work at a stall in John Street market. About three or four months ago you came to my stall and bought a whip and some crotchless knickers.' All of a sudden the Karachi curry house, where you could not have heard yourself talk, had become as quiet as a church mouse. Everyone stopped eating. The people at the front of us had turned round to see who this pervert was who had bought the crotchless knickers and the whip. I said, 'No, it wasn't me.' She said, 'It was, I would recognise you anywhere.' I had to do a bit of quick thinking here as she was talking quite loudly and everyone was listening. I said, 'I have an identical twin brother.' I had to tell a porky, to which she replied, 'Oh, I'm sorry. When you see your brother, tell him you have met the lady who served him with the whip and the crotchless knickers.'

I'll go back to Barrie Stamper, who was the director of a window company. One Saturday night we had been to the club at Greengates playing our usual game of solo, or three-card brag or poker. Although I lived only five minutes away from the club, I used to run Barrie home as he could not drive. He thus always had a chauffeur. On the way to Barrie's house he said, 'Do you fancy a fish?' Now it was after twelve o'clock and the fish shops shut at eleven o'clock, so I said, 'You will not get a fish at this time of night, they are all closed.' Barrie said, 'I'll bet you £10 I can get two fish.' I thought this a safe bet. The fish shops must have been closed for at least one and a quarter hours, so I accepted. At the time you could get a fish for fifteen old pennies. I thought I was on a safe bet when Barrie said, 'Pull up there outside that fish shop.' The fish shop was closed and had a closed sign on the door and they were cleaning up. I said to Barrie, 'You have no chance, they are closed.' Barrie knocked on the door window and the guy said, 'Sorry, we are closed.' Gary said, 'I only want two fish and I will pay you a fiver for each.' It wasn't difficult to imagine what the fish shop owner would be thinking: two fish for ten pounds? He would have to cut, batter and fry 150 fish for that sort of money.

The guy opened up his shop, setting the pan going so it had to warm up. Fifteen minutes later Barrie came out with two fresh and very hot fish. We sat in the car and made a meal of them.

'Well done, Barrie, I don't know how you pulled that one off.'

To which Barrie said, 'Well, I offered him five pounds for each fish and you bet me a tenner, so thanks for the fish – you owe me a tenner.' So I paid up. One of the nicest fish I have had, and definitely one of the most expensive.

One Saturday night, after playing cards, we had passed the fish shop that opened for the right price. But this time it was closed, and no lights on. We went to a place called Pie Albert's. Now this place stayed open until 2 a.m. and served pie and peas. Barrie said, 'Do you fancy pie and peas?' We had been drinking since 8 p.m. and it was now one forty-five. I was hungry and said yes, so in we went to Pie Albert's.

We both ordered pie and peas. It was busy, so we sat down. The owner or manager came over to our table and said, 'It will be about ten to fifteen minutes, is that OK?' We said it would, and he stopped and talked to us for five minutes. He asked me if I had been far that day. I said, 'Yes, I've been down the motorway to Bury-Bolton and Manchester and back.' He said, 'Do you do a lot of travelling then?'

'Yes, all the time.' End of conversation. Our food had arrived. I started on the pie and peas, had a couple of mouthfuls (yes, there was some still left) and the bottom of the pie was rock hard. It had been warmed up that many times you would have needed a power saw to get through it.

Now I didn't need any Dutch courage inside me to give him a piece of my mind, but when I have had a drink I am worse – and I was well oiled. I took the pie and peas up to the counter, told them I wouldn't feed such stuff to a starving dog (and I don't like dogs) and I threw the pie and peas over the counter. It hit the back wall above the cooker and I said I would never go in there again.

Three years later I fancied some pie and peas. I was passing Pie Albert's and I thought, It's three years ago. He will have forgotten the incident if he's still there. So in I went, ordered pie and peas and sat down. The guy who brought my pie and peas said, 'Hi there, are you still going up and down the motorway to Bury and Bolton?' He never said a thing about the stale pie and peas being thrown behind the counter.

Silly Things Said and Done

I suppose everyone can look back over the years at silly little things they have done or said, and I am no different. So here are a few of mine that I can remember.

When I was about nine years old I used to play out with Keith Stocks. He was a few years older than me, and there was nothing he dared not do. He enjoyed doing things that no one else would even think about. A particular time I remember was when we used to go blackberry picking in Fagley Woods. We would set off with empty Ostermilk tins, which were quite big. To give you some idea of the size, you could empty two full bags of sugar into the tin and close the lid quite easily.

The blackberry bushes at the side of the road were the easiest to get to, but they had only a few ripe berries. The ones you couldn't get to were full of big, juicy blackberries. This was a challenge to Keith Stocks. These were a long way down from the top of the quarry, which had water in the bottom that was very deep. From the bushes it was a good 100 foot drop to the water. To get to the top of the quarry you had to climb a high wall. On the other side was a small ledge that had a few blackberry bushes on. Then it was down the side of the quarry.

Keith climbed down and said to me, 'Come on down here. There's loads of really big ones.'

'What if I fall?' I said.

Keith said, 'You'll only land in the water.'

I reminded Keith that I could not swim properly. It was a good four lengths of a swimming bath before you hit land, and I could only swim the breadth of the bath. 'I'll dive in and get you out,' said Keith. Because I had a lot of faith in him I climbed down the quarry to pick those big, juicy blackberries. Each week it got easier, but I was glad when the blackberry-picking season was over.

When we didn't go into Fagley Woods we would go down to Laisterdyke station. The steam trains stopped here on their way from Bradford to Leeds. To gain access to the platforms, you had to go down the steps from the bridge that spanned all the lines.

On the outside of this covered bridge was a wood plinth that stuck out about one foot. The dare was to climb over the wall on to this plinth, get to where the trains came under the bridge, and stand there on the plinth until a train came thundering past – that's if it wasn't stopping at the station. You would be as black as the ace of spades with all the soot that came out of the funnel from the train's furnace. The stationmaster was never happy with us, but he could not catch us. We were too quick for him.

Next to the station was a mill that had its own dam. The only way you could get round this dam was to put your feet on the top of the sloping dam wall. This was attached to the main building and was the width of a red brick, i.e. three or four inches. You put your back to the mill wall, turned your feet round so the outside of your clogs or boots was touching the wall, and gingerly walked your way round the dam without falling in. Keith used to say, 'It doesn't matter if you fall in whether you can swim or not, as the water is boiling and you would be boiled alive.' I believed him – well, I was only nine.

Another adventure I had with Keith was climbing up the drainpipes and on to the school roof to retrieve all the balls that had been knocked there when the schoolkids were playing their games. The idea was to get up on the roof before the caretaker put his ladder up and did the same as we did, and keep the balls. When he saw us he would put his ladder up and chase us over the roofs, but he never caught us as we could climb down a drainpipe quicker that he could move his ladder. He dared not climb down a drainpipe, and we knew this.

When I went to Tyersal School, I was twelve years old. Because it was 'mixed' boys and girls, you sometimes saw more of the girls than you were supposed to when they were changing into their PT gear. You could see a bit more if you looked through the glass window. One day they were getting changed and we were waiting to go into the class opposite the girls' changing room. There was one girl, whose name was Mary, who would be about fourteen years of age, and she had a very large bust for her age. One of my mates – I think it was Harry Long – said, 'I dare you to go in there and tweak Mary's bust,' or something like that. Now, little Harold Perkins never ducked out of a dare. I used to think if you ducked out of a dare you were a yellow-bellied chicken. So in I went, straight up to Mary, and tweaked her. For this I got slapped on the face and received six of the best from the Headmaster. To this day I can't remember if it was worth it.

As I got into my thirties, I didn't get any better. I stopped doing the dares, but still did the silly things. I once played three-card brag for two days and nights on the trot. At the end of it I had lost my suit and my Italian shoes and had to borrow a pair of jeans, a jumper and shoes that were three sizes too big for me. I was getting dafter.

Not quite as daft, though, as when we had been to an all-night party at our Susie's house in Idle village. By the time it got to the early hours I was getting a bit the worse for wear. They were all saying I was over the hill. At the time I would have been about thirty-five and quite fit, so I said, 'I can run, jump, f— or fight better than anyone in here, and I'll have the women out first.' None of the women took me up on my challenge and none of the men, so all that was left was the running. Idle village was about six miles from where we lived and I said I would run home, even though it was four in the morning and belting it down with rain. Sandra said, 'Don't be silly and get in the car.' I told her to drive home and I would run home. When I got to the roundabout at Five Lane Ends, Sandra was waiting in the car. I waved her on and said I would stick to my word and run home. After I had run down King's Road to the lights she was waiting again. Once more I waved her on. Next came Queen's Road, a very steep hill. I thought, When I get to the top of this hill I'll get in the car, as I was wet through and knackered, but it wasn't to be. Sandra was not waiting for me. She had taken me at my word and driven straight home. When I eventually arrived home, exhausted and wet, I was sober. The two-and-a-half-hour run as well as the rain sobered me up, but I was still tired. I had a meeting at 9 a.m., although it was Easter Monday. By the time I had a bath and a cup of tea it was nearly time for the meeting.

At the meeting were Barrie, Frank, David and myself. Something got the better of me and I fell asleep with my head on the boardroom table. Barrie said, 'Are we keeping you up, Mr Perkins?'

In the early sixties, although I was working at Mills Scaffolding, I also worked Friday, Saturday and Sunday night as a waiter in a pub called the Junction. It was a very busy place. I started at seven thirty, put my white waiter's coat on, put my one pound and ten shilling float in my pocket, got my free half of beer and that was it. I never stopped all night. I didn't have time to drink my free half. Last drinks were at ten thirty. Normally with the clearing up and a bit of cleaning up I was done for eleven o'clock. My pay was ten shillings a night (50p). I even remember the price of the beer. Bitter was one shilling and a halfpenny, mixed was one shilling, and mild was eleven pence halfpenny a pint. As most people were regulars I knew what their round was as soon as they came through the door.

When I first started there were two of us waiting on. We waited on the tap room, the singing room, the lounge, the snug and even on people who were sat in the bar room, who only had to take two or three steps and they would be at the bar. No, you had to serve them.

All the rooms and the bar had little buttons on the wall. When the customers wanted a drink they pressed the button. At the side of the bar was a box with flaps on. If the tap room rang, the flap with 'Tap Room' on it would drop down, and off you would go to see who wanted serving. After I had been there four weeks, the landlord said to me, 'I have been watching you this last few weeks and I think you could do this job on your own.' I thought that if I was doing two men's work I would at least get another fifteen shillings or a pound more a week. My fault for not asking. But when the end of Sunday night's shift came, I just got my normal one pound ten shilling for three shifts. I wasn't very happy, but I kept going on my own for another six or seven weeks. It was hard work. Not only did I not have time to drink my free half of beer, I didn't have time to scratch my bum.

The crunch came on a Sunday night. I was running round like a blue-arsed fly. Everyone wanted a drink at the same time. I took a round of drinks into the tap room and the four lads playing dominoes said, 'Same again, Harold.' I knew the round: three pints of bitter and a pint of mixed. One of the guys who usually drank bitter said he wanted a bottle of stout, so I said, 'Two bitters, one mixed and a bottle of stout?' The guy who was drinking the mixed, who was a little bit drunk as he had been drinking all Sunday afternoon and night, said, 'Get him a pint.' The guy who wanted the stout said, 'No, I want a stout.' The guy whose round it was, who was drunk, said, 'I'm paying – get him a pint.'

I thought, I am too busy to stand here listening to this crap when other people are waiting to be served. So I went to the bar and ordered two bitters, one mixed and a bottle of stout. I thought, if this guy wants a bottle of stout he can have one. When I went back to the tap room I put the mixed down on the table first, then the two pints of bitter. I was just about to put the stout down on the table when the guy whose round it was said, 'I told you a pint of bitter. I am not paying you for a bottle of stout.' By this time I had had enough. I picked the bottle of stout up, hit him over the head

265

with it, punched him on the nose, took my float out of my waiter's coat, threw the coat over the bar and said, 'I'm finished, I've had enough.' I walked out of the door. The end of my 'waiting on' career.

One time I was working up Thornton Road just above where Les Bellet's wife ran a transport cafe (Les Bellet was a famous wrestler). Jamie Higgins and I used to go in for breakfast. It was a brilliant breakfast, but the pots that she served the tea in needed a good scrub. One morning she gave me a pot of tea that had a brown mark on each side, so I asked for a clean pot. She gave me another one and it was the same, so I told her. She said they were all like that and it wouldn't come off. As she was talking to me she had a tea towel draped over her shoulder, so I took the towel and gave the pot a good hard rub with the damp tea towel, same on the other side, and the marks came off. I gave her the towel back and said, 'All it wants is some elbow grease and they will come clean.' I sat back down and finished my breakfast.

The next day Jamie and I went in for breakfast and all the pots were gleaming. Nothing was said, we just sat down eating our breakfasts with our nice clean pots of tea. Then in walked Les Bellet. I saw his wife point over to our table. Les Bellet came over, put both his big hands on the table and said, 'Right, who called my wife a dirty bitch?'

Straight away Jamie said, 'It wasn't me.'

I thought for a moment I was working with Sammy: 'It wasn't me.' Now, I thought, I am going through one of those two windows. I hope it's the low one, it's not as far to fall when I get to the other side. I said to Les Bellet, 'Now, just a minute. I never said she was a dirty bitch. I just told her she needed some elbow grease on those pots, and by the gleam on these pots now it must have worked.' Les Bellet, still with his two big hands on the table, raised his left arm above my head. I thought, 'Here I go, get ready, window,' but he brought his hand down and patted me on the back.

'Well done, lad, I've been telling her she's a dirty bitch for years and she's never listened to me. But she did to you, thank you.' With his left hand on my shoulder he lifted his right hand off the table, shook hands with me, then sat down and had a chat with us. 'That your car out there?' It was a big Ford with a long bonnet. I can't remember its exact model, but it got the nickname of the Dagenham Dustbin or Flying Pig. 'Yes,' I said, 'I'm just having a bit of trouble with the heater.'

'I have one the same as yours, and had the same trouble with the heater. I bet it's the thermostat,' said Les. When I said I would call for one on the way home from work, Les said, 'I'm going down to Parkinson's [Ford dealers]. I'll get you one and give you it tomorrow.' I thought, That's nice of him. One minute I thought he was going to bounce me through the window, now he's going to do a bit of shopping for me.

Harold Perkins

The next day we went in for breakfast, sat down, and Les Bellet came up with the thermostat. 'Thank you. How much do I owe you?' I said.

'Nothing,' said Les. 'Have that one on the house. You did in five minutes what I couldn't do in twenty years. You've done me a favour.' I had always been a big fan of Les Bellet. I used to watch him every time he was on the television. He was brilliant and I had met him, shook hands with him, and he bought me a thermostat for my car. A really nice guy.

One episode that does stick out in my mind was a games night at Greengates Liberal Cub. Although the club doors were locked at ten thirty, on a games night they were left open until eleven o'clock. If you were last on playing snooker you could at least get into the club to take your snooker cue back. One night, someone had locked the doors at ten thirty. I arrived back with David Lister and the team's snooker cues at ten forty-five. We knocked on the doors but, as the club was at the top of a flight of steps, the knocking fell on deaf ears.

It was a nice evening and the French windows leading to the balcony were open. Being a sprightly scaffolder I gave the snooker cues to David Lister and shinned up the drainpipe. I swung over to grab the balcony rail, leapt over through the French windows, went down the steps and opened the door for David. At the time both David and myself were serving on the committee, and I was reported to the committee for 'gaining access to the club by means of climbing up the drain pipe' – that is how it was worded. Come the next committee meeting, we were all in the small room where the meetings were held. Everything carried on as normal until it got to 'Any Other Business'. The secretary, Nathan Field, who was a very good friend of mine and a nice guy, said, 'Yes, a report of a member of the committee, namely Harold Perkins, gaining access to the club premises by means of climbing up the drainpipe.' Well, Nathan could see the funny side of this and was doing his very best to keep a straight face, but he had to look at me when he said, 'Mr Perkins, will you leave the room while we discuss this matter?' I could see him finding it very hard not to laugh; I am sure Nathan will remember that. When I returned to the committee room I was given a warning, and I had to promise not to gain access to the club that way again.

I was working with Peter Jack on a block of flats in Leeds (the one where someone burnt through the ropes on the cradles) in 1966, when the World Cup was on. Now I have never been a fan of football, rugby or cricket – I just don't know anything about football. We were coming down from the tenth floor in the lift and a man got in. You know the feeling, like being in a doctor's waiting room, no one talking. This guy said to me, 'What did you think of Eusebio last night?' I didn't want to hurt his feelings by saying I was not interested, so I thought I would be sociable. I said, 'I thought they played very well.' There was a deadly silence after that.

When the lift arrived at the ground floor, the guy went one way and Peter and I went the other. When this man was out of earshot, Peter Jack said to me, 'Eusebio is a player, you prat.' Told you I knew nothing about football.

In 1980 I fortunately came across a few thousand pairs of ladies' knickers. They were a job lot and came at the right price. I tried to sell them straight to the wholesalers, but they didn't want to know, same with the retailers. At the time car boot sales had just got going, so I thought, The first Sunday I am not working I'll do a car boot. We bought a few hundred plastic bags and started to pack the knickers according to sizes and different colours. What a surprise we got when we discovered that some of the knickers had only one leg hole, while some had two crotches or gussets. But they came at the right price, so we carried on packing and having a laugh over the deformed knickers with two or three gussets in.

The first Sunday I did a car boot sale a pal of mine called Alan gave me a hand and we were going great guns. I was shouting, 'Ladies' knickers are down today' – because I got them at the right price they could be sold at the right price. We were selling them at £2 for a pack of five and they were going like hot cakes. Some ladies even asked if they had been used, to which I said, 'Madam, if these ladies' knickers had been worn and soiled they would be selling for £10 a pack, not £2.' After five or six Sundays we got rid of them all, made a profit and I had done something I hadn't done before, a car boot sale. What a life.

I don't know whether this one comes under silly things, but I'll put it in. Barry Samuels, Peter Jack and I were working for D&A Scaffolding (it would be in the late sixties) on a church at Haxby, near York. We had to erect a scaffolding inside the church to give access to the walls and ceilings so they could be given a coat of paint.

We were working happily away. I was on the scaffold singing 'Rock around the Clock' and smoking a fag, when in came the priest. 'Stop singing!' he shouted at the top of his voice, going red in the face and slavering with the shock of hearing me sing. I had been brought up in the Catholic faith and used to go to church three times a day until I saw the light and converted to being an atheist, so I thought I would have a dig at him for being a sourpuss. Just as I was about to try to convert him to my belief, he shouted, 'You don't sing in the Lord's house!' to which I replied, 'You sing on a Sunday morning, don't you?'

He replied, 'We only sing the Lord's songs, not the trash you were singing.'

By this time he had noticed I was smoking. Sammy had shoved his cig into the end of a scaffold tube so he couldn't see him with a cigarette, but I wasn't going to hide my ciggy, not this recently converted atheist, no. So I carried on smoking and he let out another rant. 'You do not smoke in the Lord's house.' I think if I had been on the ground he would have attacked me, the way he was frothing at the mouth, eyes bulging and going red, but I was forty feet above him so I had the advantage. 'There is no smoking in the Lord's house, do you hear me?' he ranted again. I carried on working and smoking and he carried on ranting. 'There is no smoking in this church, do you hear me?'

I said, 'What about when you waft that jug about with all the scent inside, that smokes doesn't it?' By this time he had had enough of me and reported me to the boss. I got a slight telling off.

So it was no smoking, no singing and there were no toilets. When we wanted a leak we went round to the boiler room steps and that was our loo. One Monday morning just after we had our break at ten, Peter Jack said to me, 'I need a toilet.' I told him to use the boiler room steps. He said, 'I can't, I will be using paper.' We weren't on good terms with the priest. I couldn't see him allowing Peter to use his house toilet so I went round to the boiler house, opened the door and inside was a pile of coal, a big shovel and a roaring fire in the boiler. I suggested that he should put part of his Daily Mirror on the big shovel, do what he had to do, open the furnace door, throw the lot in then insert the shovel back into the pile of coal. So he did what he had to do, then came back inside the church.

Now directly above the boiler room was the place where they guzzle their wine on the side. After about five minutes the priest came out. Sammy and I were up on the scaffold and Peter was on the deck just outside the wine-guzzling place when the priest came out. He stood next to Peter and said, 'Can you smell something?' He replied, 'Yes, Father, it smells like something's burning.' The priest replied, 'Smells like something's burning? It smells like someone has died.' Sammy and I up on the scaffold couldn't stop laughing, and Peter was nipping himself so he didn't laugh.

We were at the Waggoner's pub in Queensbury at a fancy dress party. Every year Kenny Brady used to spend all day dressing himself up, and he did a good job of it. One year he would dress up as the Incredible Hulk and paint all his body in green paint. One year he came as a fisherman or trawlerman, and came with all the wet suit and the sou'wester. He had bought ten packets of Fisherman's Friends. It was unusual for Kenny to spend money, as he is a bit careful with his pennies. He would be going round the pub giving his Fisherman's Friends out and playing a recording of a ship's foghorn on his small mobile tape recorder.

He was stood in the corner with the regular crowd when he said, 'I think I've eaten too many of those Fisherman's Friends. I think I will have to go to the toilet double quick.' While he was sat on the bog, Peter Jack and I filled a bucket with water, about three gallons, and went into the gents.

We knocked on the toilet door and said, 'Are you still in there?'

He replied, 'Yes, I'll be a few minutes yet.' At that we threw the bucket of water over the top of the door and ran. When he came out of the toilet and stood at the bar, he said, 'I was glad I left my sou'wester on.' Kenny didn't know, but round the rim of his southwester was about half a pint of water. When he looked down to see where his pint was, the water went into his beer, much to the amusement of everyone except Kenny.

One evening Sandra and I were having a tour round the pubs. We called in a pub in Bingley called the Ferrands Arms. We were stood at the bar having a chat when in came eight Hell's Angels with their leather gear and riding boots on. They sat down with their beer about ten feet from where we were stood at the bar. Everything was OK until they started effing and blinding. Although I swear, I never swear when ladies are present, and I don't like it. So I walked over to these eight Hell's Angels and said, 'Excuse me, lads, there is a lady in my company and she can hear you swearing. Can you just button your lips on swearing, OK?' With that I walked back to the bar, thinking, That was a stupid move to make. I'll probably end up through one of those windows head first. There was a deathly silence. I thought the best thing I could do was leg it. So I said to Sandra, 'Sup up, we're going.' We finished our drinks and went out of the door. The car park was across from the pub and I could see their motor bikes parked just in front of my car. We were about forty feet from the car when I heard this voice: 'Excuse me.' I turned round and it was the Hell's Angels. I thought, This is it. I told Sandra to get in the car. Seconds later a hand came on my shoulder. I was thinking, I've no chance. I'll hit this guy then jump in the car before his mates get hold of me. Once I'm in the car, if they start anything I'll run them down, bikes and all.

I spun round ready to lamp this guy and he said to me, 'We are all sorry for swearing and upsetting your wife, and we apologise.' With that he put his hand out and we shook hands. What a relief. I thought, I will have to learn to keep my gob shut.

I think nearing the end of her days my Mother had lost her memory or just didn't want to know me.

Sandra and myself were at a family funeral, we went to sit down in the chapel and I ended up sitting next to Alfred May who was in turn sat next to my Mother. I let on to Alfred May and had a short chat to him, then he turned to my Mother and said

"Have you seen who's here?"

To this my Mother said

"Who"

Alfred May said

"It's Harold"

With this said my Mother leaned forward and looked at me, she said to Alfred May

"Harold who?"

Well I thought this was funny it caught my weird sense of humour and I started to chuckle to myself, so when Sandra asked what I was laughing about I told her and she thought it was funny but said

"You can't laugh at a funeral"

Sail Away

When we first started in the scaffolding we didn't take any holidays. Not only could we not afford them, we just didn't have the time as we were working seven days a week every week. So we went for four years before we had a holiday. Even then it was only for a week, but things would get better, and they did.

We were out one Saturday night having a drink with some friends, Teddy and Jean Leach. Teddy said to me, 'Have you ever been on a cruise ship?' We had thought about it but never taken the final step. Teddy and Jean had been on a few cruises and said that we would like it, so we booked to go on a ship called the Dynasty with Teddy and Jean. This ship sailed out of Fort Lauderdale in America.

While we were in Fort Lauderdale, we stopped in a hotel called the Almond Tree. It was supposed to be a four-star, but my rating was a one-star. We went down for breakfast and they served us tea in a dirty cup (yes, I did think of Les Bellet's wife). The tea was lukewarm, and the second cup they brought was also dirty, so I refused to eat there. Teddy said they had been to a diner over the road and it looked clean and tidy but they had only had a drink, nothing to eat. Off we went over the road to this American diner. We ordered hot tea for two and I ordered bacon, egg, tomatoes and a slice of toast. Sandra ordered scrambled egg on toast. Sandra's came, scrambled egg on toast with bacon on top. I thought, When you order scrambled egg they must treat you to a couple of rashers of bacon. Wrong. When mine came it was two eggs, no bacon and two slices of cold tomato. By this time Sandra had eaten the bacon so I thought, Never mind, I don't like cold tomatoes with breakfast but I have two nice-looking eggs. I am going to enjoy these with my lukewarm tea and cold toast. Wrong. I dipped a piece of toast into the egg yolk and it was cold – not lukewarm, it was cold. I thought, Don't say anything. I just won't come here again.

I was sipping my lukewarm tea when the waitress came up, looked at the plate and saw the two eggs were still there. She said, 'Is there something wrong, sir?' When I told her the reason they were still there was because they were cold, she said, 'They couldn't be cold, sir. Were yours cold, madam?' Sandra said that her meal, with my bacon, was OK. I said to the waitress that if the meal had been warm I would have eaten it, but it was cold, and I wouldn't say it was cold if it was not. At that she stuck her fingers in the egg yolks and said, 'They may be cold now, sir, but they were hot when I put them on the table.'

That was the straw that broke the camel's back. I went to the counter and asked for the bill. Sat at the counter were about eight people dining. Once again, she said, 'They were hot when they came out.' By this time I had got the right amount of dollars to pay the bill. I got hold of her by the wrist with one hand and with my other hand slapped the bill and the money in her hand. I kept hold of her by the wrist and said to her, 'Here and don't ever f—ing talk to me like that again.' I walked out of a very quiet diner.

We were in Fort Lauderdale for a couple of nights before we boarded the ship, so we thought we would explore the night life. I always thought that if you are in a place you don't know, it's a good idea to ask a taxi driver, as they should know all the good and bad places to go. So we said to a cab driver, 'Do you know a decent bar? Not a grotty one, somewhere nice.'

'Sure,' said the cab driver. 'Sinatra's bar.'

So off we headed for Sinatra's bar. We paid the cab driver, walked up some steps into the bar and sat down on some very low seats and an even lower table. Along came a very tall, good-looking dusky maiden with a micro-miniskirt who took our order for drinks. When she returned to our table with the tray of drinks she squatted down and took her time putting the drinks on the table, much to the delight of Teddy and myself. We discovered that all she was wearing was the micro-miniskirt. When she had finished serving the drinks she said to Teddy and me, 'Would you like anything else, sir?'

The first stop on the cruise was Cozumel in Mexico. The thing I remember about Cozumel was the traffic lights. The system consisted of a policeman holding two table tennis bats. One was red and the other green. When he wanted to stop the traffic he held the red bat up above his head and waved to the pedestrians with the green bat. Then, when all the pedestrians had crossed the road, he reversed the order, holding and waving the green bat above his head, with the red bat at waist height pointing to pedestrians — a little bit ancient, but it worked very well.

The other thing I remember about Cozumel was Teddy saying, 'Let's find a decent bar and have a drink.' We walked along the front and finally came to a bar and Teddy said, 'Let's go in here.'

I said, 'We can't — there's a sign saying "Members Only".'

Teddy said, 'Yes, and there's another one saying "Everyone Welcome".'

So we went in. All I can remember about the bar was that it had wood shavings on the floor and all the tables and stools were shaped like nuts and bolts.

Our next stop was Grand Cayman Island, a very beautiful place. On the island they have a submarine that takes you down to the bottom of the ocean. With the water being very clear, even at 100 feet down you can see everything around you. It cost a few quid to go down in it, but was worth every penny – a spectacular sight. Next stop we went round the turtle farm, another great scene. We visited a place called Hell. They had some tourist shops and a post office where you could buy post cards and get them stamped to say they had been sent from Hell. A short path led on to a bridge where you looked out on to large black spikes. Apparently someone had seen these years ago and said, 'If there is a place called Hell, I bet it looks like this.' So this is how it got its name.

Then on we sailed to the Panama Canal. It took us eight or nine hours to go through the canal. It was a wonderful education to see those huge ships being lifted up and down in the locks. I can certainly recommend it – it was brilliant.

We called at San José, which was another attractive town, before we ended up in Acapulco. On the seafront you have all the posh hotels and the glitz, and a stone's throw away down the back streets you can see pigs running in and out of houses where people are living. Two completely different views within half a mile.

We all got in a taxi and the driver gave us a tour showing us where all the big stars used to go and stay. Of course, we ended up at the only place to end up in Acapulco: a ringside seat to watch the people who dive off the cliff. They start from the bottom part of the cliff, then work their way up to the finale, the top board. We were sat in a little alcove where we had a brilliant view of the diver limbering up and making the sign of the cross before he made his dive. As soon as he hit the water we were up and out of our alcove seat and heading for the lift, which was only four or five minutes. As we came through the door leading to the lift this guy was stood there in his swimming trunks dripping wet through, holding a container out for you to put money in. I thought, Just a minute, he's dived from the top of that cliff, swum to the shore, and he's got here before us. I think he must have had a double and they were keeping him in a cupboard with his trunks on. As soon as the diver hit the water they pulled him out, threw a bucket of water over him and stood him next to the lift hoping to collect some money.

The only time I did something as good as going down in the submarine was in Tenerife. We were on holiday with my daughter Stacey and her husband, Tony. We saw an advert to go 'bobcatting'. I was intrigued as to what this bobcatting was, so we went up and read the advert. It consisted of getting on a boat that held about ten people and these bobcats. They take you out to sea to a spot where it is about twenty-five feet deep. Once at the spot, the bobcats are put into the sea. They are like a little scooter with a big goldfish-type bowl on top. This is filled with air. After you have put on a wetsuit, you have to get into the sea and swim to where the bobcats are, about thirty feet away from the boat. You have to take a deep breath, put your head under the water and put your head into the goldfish-like bowl.

On the way to the diving site we had been shown all the communication signs, like up, down, OK, etc. so we could communicate while we were on the seabed. I was first down and was told not to move from my spot until all the others were down. I went down to the seabed and sat on my bobcat. The diver gave me the OK sign and I returned it. He gestured to me to stay put and I gave him the OK sign again and sat there looking round at all the different coloured fish. Telling me to stay put in a situation like that was like asking a baby not to cry, so while the diver was bringing the next guy down I set off on my own to explore the deep blue sea. It was brilliant. You turned the throttle and it sent the propeller round at the back of the bobcat and whizzed you forward. When you turned the handlebars it worked the rudder that turned you right or left. I was really enjoying myself until the diver came down and saw I wasn't on my spot. Did I get a telling off for not obeying the 'stay there' rule!

When the rest of the team came down we went in posse style with one diver in front and one behind. One of the divers lifted a rock up and pulled out a baby octopus and beckoned me to hold my hands out to hold the octopus, which I did – it was brilliant. It was like being on another planet, whizzing round the ocean bed looking at things you had not seen before.

The next time I went on a bobcat there was a lady on board. She asked me if I had done this before. I told her I had, and how good it was. She said she was looking forward to it, and said to me, 'It doesn't matter if you can't swim does it?' I just didn't believe anyone who could not swim would have the guts to jump in the sea and then go down on the seabed. I thought she was pulling my leg, but no – she told the divers she could not swim. After looking at one another in amazement, they lowered her over the side of the boat and, with one diver on either side of her, swam with her to the bobcat, where she was told to take a deep breath. They then shoved her head down into the water and up into the goldfish bowl. I just didn't believe what I was seeing. When she came up the divers again helped her to the side of the boat and back into it. On the way back, she said to me, 'That was incredible.' I thought she was incredible: a very brave lady.

The first time we went to Australia we went via Singapore. My old mate Raymond Sutton and his wife, Lena, flew over to Singapore to meet us. They were staying at the Boulevard Hotel on Orchard Grove, and we were staying at the River View in Chinatown. We were there for three nights before flying to Brisbane on the same flight as Raymond and his wife.

Raymond and Lena were waiting in the foyer of our hotel when we arrived. The hotel was lovely and the young staff spoke excellent English, with an American accent, and were very polite, I remember the first morning we went down for breakfast and ordered two poached eggs on toast. When they came they had been poached just right – they were perfect, which is unusual in a hotel. By the time they arrive at the table they are usually hard and cold. Not believing they could serve them perfectly again we ordered the same the next morning. Sure enough they came perfectly poached again. I later found out that the reason they spoke with an American accent was from watching the American movies on video in order to improve their English.

As it was our first time in Singapore we relied on Raymond and his new wife, Lena, to show us round. He had been there a few times and knew the places to go, like the warehouse where you could buy a 'Gucci' watch for seven Singapore dollars. Mine lasted me for two years before it conked out on me, although the taxi driver did say take it off when you wash your hands. I must have forgotten. But it was a good buy for seven dollars.

We flew from Singapore to Brisbane on a night flight, and Sandra and I were the only ones awake. To save us pressing the button that went 'ping' every time we wanted a drink, the stewardess asked if it was OK to bring us two vodkas and tonic every twenty to thirty minutes to save us disturbing people – the answer was yes.

We stayed with Raymond and Lena for three weeks. She is from the Philippines and a very likable lady. I think all the English women had had enough of

Raymond, so he had to cast his net further afield. Raymond had a big place and he used to boast that his lawn was that big he had to buy a tractor to cut it.

One day Sandra was doing some ironing when she stood on a frog and screamed. It was squashed under her foot – ugh! Raymond said it was the frog season and if you left a door or a window open in they came without an invitation. The same night we went out for a meal and had a few drinks. We came back to Raymond and Lena's and had a few more drinks and a chinwag and retired to the sack about two thirty. I was fast asleep when I got a smack round the chops followed by, 'You dirty bastard, what do you think you're doing?' Sandra had been asleep, and a frog had jumped on her face. Now, what she thought I was doing I don't know, but I caught the frog after about ten minutes and threw it out of the window. It was only when I showed her the frog she realised it was the frog on her face and not me.

We went down to Surfers' Paradise for a few days on our own. We booked into a hotel that looked out on to the beautiful Pacific Ocean. It had glass windows all the way round and if you went down in the lift to the basement you opened a door and you were on the lovely white sandy beach. It was absolutely brilliant. We drove down in a Triumph car that was lent to us by a guy who used to live in Huddersfield. We just started talking to him while we were having a drink and mentioned that we were going to hire a car to drive down to Surfers' Paradise, and he said, 'I've got a spare car you can take.' He wouldn't take any money for the hire, so I got it serviced and had some new windscreen wipers fitted for him. You don't come across many people like that. We went back a week later to Surfers' Paradise for another few days in the same hotel because we liked the night life down there.

We went to see Sandra's cousin Maureen and her family in Brisbane for a day, and then we flew up to Cairns for three days. We had a trip to Green Island on the Barrier Reef and ate the biggest prawns you have ever seen.

Then it was a flight back to the UK via Hong Kong. Now, that's a sight to see, landing at Hong Kong airport at night. You can see all the skyscrapers lit up and they are so close you think you will hit them – breathtaking.

Another ship we went on with Teddy and Jean was the Marco Polo. This ship sailed out of Singapore through the South China Sea and our first port of call was Java, where we visited a place called Semarang. To get to Semarang from where the ship docked it was normally a three-and-a-half- to four-hours' coach drive because of the slow-moving traffic. But not in our case. We were given a police escort from the ship to Semarang. The police wouldn't let anything overtake us. We had an escort of four police bikes. Two would go in front. When we came to the traffic lights, they would stop all the traffic while we got through. If there was any traffic in front of us the police waved them to the side of the road so we could get past. The four-hour journey was done in one-and-a-half hours. We felt like royalty.

We were given a conducted tour of the local town hall by the mayor and taken to see the temple at Semarang, which we were told had been buried for hundreds of years and had only recently been unearthed. The views on the way to Semarang were spectacular. You could see the locals bathing in the streams and doing their washing.

After Java we sailed to Bali – again a very picturesque place. We were there for only half a day and I was under the weather, so I don't remember a lot about the place. I do remember two Americans who must have been eighty or ninety years old squaring up to one another in an argument over queue jumping. That was the highlight of the day.

Our first port of call in Australia was Darwin, where we tried to buy some duty-free vodka. But it was very expensive because they were trying to make it unobtainable to the locals. Also, we found out you were not allowed to take alcohol back on to the ship.

We then sailed through the Great Barrier Reef to Cairns and called at Hamilton Island, which is part of the Whitsunday Islands. This place is just like looking at a picture postcard. The only form of transport apart from a push bike was a golf buggy. Yes, no buses or cars, just a battery-powered golf buggy to get you round.

By the time we arrived at Hamilton Island we had been sailing for about two weeks. The food on board ship was very good, but we were dying for a portion of fish and chips. You can imagine my delight when Sandra said, 'Look, a fish and chip shop.' I thought the last place you would find a fish shop would be on Hamilton Island. I joined the queue and placed my order for fish and chips twice. We sat down outside and ate our fish and chips on the beautiful Hamilton Island. Delicious.

Next call was Brisbane. We had a full day there and Sandra's cousin Maureen and her son David came down to the ship to see us. We showed them round the ship and they thought it was wonderful. We spent a couple of days in Sydney, which is a great place to be. It's really buzzing with life. Then it was back to Manchester airport via Hong Kong, no stop-over. What a great holiday.

We took a three-day cruise from Limassol, Cyprus to Egypt and Israel – a whistle-stop tour, but well worth doing. We were getting off the ship at five o'clock in the morning. In order to get ashore you had to walk on this pontoon bridge. At the end of the bridge, just before you put your feet on terra firma, there were about a dozen stalls selling trinkets and leather goods. At five o'clock in the morning the last thing I want is a guy with a fez on his head grabbing hold of my arm and literally trying to drag me to his stall to buy something that I don't want. It's not that I'm bad-tempered at five o'clock in the morning, but after asking him not to grab me by the arm a couple of times I told him if he did that again I would thump him one. Needless to say he grabbed hold of my arm and I went to thump him. Security must have heard the commotion. They came running over, picked him up, and dragged him off. All he could say as the police dragged him away was, 'What is your mother?' I said to Sandra 'Do you really think he knows my mother?'

Another time Sandra and I were on a ship called the Statendam that was cruising the Caribbean. Teddy and Jean were on a ship called the Victoria. After about a week's sailing, both ships came into Barbados on the same day, so we met up with them for a drink. I can always remember sitting outside this little bar on a white plastic chair. Just where Jean was sat there was a step that went down about nine inches. When Jean moved her chair back her head went back her legs went up and caught under the table, and the first thing Teddy thought of doing was to save his drink, which he did. Jean was on the floor while Teddy still had his drink intact. We did eventually pick her up. We met up with them a few days later when we were both in St Lucia, and again stopped for a couple of drinks.

We once went to Cyprus with Teddy and Jean, a last-minute job. I think we booked on Wednesday and flew on Friday. We had asked to be in accommodation in Limassol or Paphos. It was allocation on arrival, but we were assured we would be stopping in Paphos. When we landed in Larnaca and the coach headed north to Protaras, a good two hours' drive to Paphos in the south, we thought, This is going to be a long journey. When we asked the representative about this, she said, 'Everyone on this coach is stopping in Protaras.' We were dropped off at a hotel with a couple who had a little boy about ten years old. They booked in first, then our turn came. They had booked us into a two-bedroomed apartment with a shared bathroom and toilet and kitchen instead of separate apartments. Nobody liked the idea of waiting to use the toilet or bath.

Teddy looked at me and said, 'You thinking same as me?' I said, 'Yes, we'll hire a car and drive down to Paphos.' So we asked the receptionist for a car hire firm and ordered a taxi to take us there. While we were waiting for the taxi, the couple who had booked in before us with the ten-year-old came to reception and asked why they were in one room and their son was in a separate room on his own. I thought, That is typical – we wanted separate rooms and they wanted a shared one. So I told them that as we were on our way to Paphos they could have our shared room.

Off we went down to Paphos to find somewhere to stay. Easier said than done. It was the busy season and all the hotels were booked. We must have tried twenty hotels in Paphos with no luck. After about two-and-a-half to three hours, I said to Teddy, 'Try this one. You may have better luck than me.' Teddy went into the Cyprius Maris hotel and came out ten minutes later with a smile on his face. 'Want the good news or the bad news first?' Well, the good news was they had just two rooms, or should I say suites – they were called the presidential suites. The reason they were vacant was they wanted 190 Cyprus pounds each suite per night. So the good news was we had somewhere to stay, the bad news was the cost. Per night, per suite, with the exchange rate at the time, it worked out at £220. So I went into the hotel with Teddy and we negotiated with the hotel manager. He reduced the price for us. So we stopped in the presidential suite for a week in complete luxury. The bath was that big that if you wanted a bath at eight o'clock you had to turn the taps on at seven o'clock. Despite the expense we had a very good holiday.

We fell in love with Cyprus and eventually bought a place in Paphos. It was nice to be able to jump on a plane without lugging the suitcases with you and know you didn't have to wait three quarters of an hour at the other end to collect your luggage.

When we visited New Zealand it was our retirement treat. We had sold the scaffolding business and, as we had both worked very hard, this trip was going to be the icing on top of the cake. We flew business class to Singapore and spent four days in the Raffles hotel in a suite. It was their rainy season, and when it rains in Singapore, it's monsoon weather. We were sat outside in the courtyard having a drink one afternoon when the heavens opened. We were at a table that had a parasol over it, so it acted as an umbrella for a while. Within sixty seconds a waiter came over to us armed with an umbrella and a shawl. He put the shawl round Sandra's shoulders, held the brolly, and beckoned us to follow him quickly. He guided us to the side of the bar where there was a canopy to shelter under. Then I realised why he wanted us to move quickly. Within four or five minutes the place where we had been sat down was awash with water rushing down towards the drain, and it was five to six inches deep. A very good service in Raffles, and also really good and polite waiters.

While we were in Raffles hotel, Sandra went to look in the Lladró shop and bought a rather expensive ornament. When it was on display it didn't look too big, but when we went back to the shop to pick it up it had grown ten times bigger because of all the packing that went round it for protection. There was no way it would go in a case. I said, 'We are not trailing that round New Zealand and Australia.' Sandra found the cure. We would leave the ornament at the Lladró shop and collect it on the way back three weeks later. This we had not planned for – another three days' stop in Raffles on the way back. That Lladró had just gone up in price.

The doorman at Raffles was a very tall guy with a turban on his head and all the fancy glitter on his jacket. One time as we were coming out of the hotel he opened the door for us, put his hand to his mouth and gave a very discreet cough, nodding his head at the same time. I had forgotten to zip my fly up. So I zipped up and said, 'Thank you,' and added, 'Dead birds don't fall out of cages.' Eventually he saw the funny side of it.

The next day when we walked past him he put his thumb up and said, 'Dead birds.'

When we called at Raffles three weeks later on our way back to the UK, on the door at Raffles was that very tall guy with the turban on his head. He came over to open the taxi door and said, 'Welcome to Raffles. Have you been here before?' I replied, 'Yes, three weeks ago. You must remember – dead birds don't fall out of cages.' The doorman just looked bewildered. I explained to him that we had been there three weeks before and that he had told me my fly was open and I had said, 'Dead birds do not fall out of cages.' He said, 'Maybe, sir, but it was not me three weeks ago. I was on holiday. It must have been my twin brother.' It could only happen to me.

We flew business class again from Singapore to Auckland on New Zealand Airways – not as luxurious as Singapore Airline but better than being in peasant class. We stayed in a nice hotel in Auckland for three nights before boarding the ship. The suite we had booked on the Statendam (our second cruise on this ship) was an 'owner's suite' and complete luxury it was. It took up nearly half of the stern of the ship and the balcony was massive. There's no other way to live. We had our own maid who brought us fresh flowers, free champagne and fresh fruit and booze. You just could not wish for better.

Our first port of call was Napier, a very quaint little place. We spent half a day there, then off to

Wellington, Picton, Christchurch, then Dunedin. I think they were originally going to call it Dundee, because there are a lot of Scottish descendants there, but for some reason they called it Dunedin.

After leaving Dunedin we stopped at the Milford Sound, a massive waterfall coming down the mountain and into the sea. We were on deck having a drink with a couple we had got friendly with and they said, 'I think we have got the best view on the ship.' I agreed, until we went back to our suite and found out our suite was right opposite the falls. We had the best view from our suite but we didn't know until we got back from the bar. Then ten minutes later we set sail.

After Milford Sound it was Tasmania. We docked at Burnie – again a little place with friendly people and very clean and tidy. From here we went to Adelaide, Melbourne, and ended up in Sydney. We stopped in the Four Seasons hotel on, I think, the fourteenth floor and from there we could see the ship we had just been on, the Opera House and Sydney Harbour Bridge. We stayed in Sydney for three days. We had booked our flights one-way as we were not sure when we wanted to go back. Sandra normally books the hotels and the flights, but this time I said, 'Leave it to me.' We went into a travel agent's and I told the girl behind the counter that if she gave us a very good price for a flight from Sydney to Brisbane, then Brisbane to Singapore, then Singapore to the UK, we would give her the booking there and then. But it would have to be good as we had had other prices (I lied). She came up with a price that was less than half of what we paid going out and we were getting an extra flight in to boot, so, yes, she got the deal.

Off we went from Sydney to Brisbane. We spent a few days in Brisbane. We called to see Sandra's cousin Maureen and her family again. Then it was back to the UK via four days at Raffles in Singapore to pick up the Lladró. I think that will go down as 'the best'.

We finally sold the company and moved to Cyprus permanently. We have no regrets. We are now both retired and comfortable on the money side so we can do what we like – go on holiday, take a cruise... Since we have been in Cyprus we have met some very nice people who you can have a laugh and a joke with – especially Nigel and June – and we have met some nasty people, but that's life.

If I had the chance of waving a magic wand to change any part of my life I wouldn't change one second – not even the time I got kicked down the cellar steps, or the backhander I received from the nightwatchman.